COMMERCIAL VEHICLES ARC

CW00735322

THE LEYLAND OC

by Graham Edge

ACKNOWLEDGEMENTS

The input of Neil Mitchell to this title, and indeed the Commercial Vehicles Archive Series, is vital for information and photographs. Neil spends many hours searching the British Commercial Vehicle Museum Archives for suitable material and details, and his unstinting efforts are here for everyone to appreciate. Mike Sutcliffe, also respectfully known as 'The Leyland Man,' advised on early Octopus models and provided several informative data sheets. Tony Petch and Rufus Carr provided photographs of Leyland Octopuses in service in Australia and New Zealand. I record my grateful thanks to these contributors and others who have imparted knowledge over many years.

Photographic Credits

Most of the photographs reproduced in this book are official Leyland Motors (and its successors) material. The negatives are in the care of the British Commercial Vehicle Museum Trust Archives. Any other photographs used have been duly accredited in the caption. Every effort has been made to trace all original copyright holders if there was any doubt.

The Commercial Vehicles Archive Series is produced and published by Gingerfold Publications in conjunction with the British Commercial Vehicle Museum Trust Archives.

This title was first published in October 2004 by Gingerfold Publications, 8, Tothill Road, Swaffham Prior, Cambridge, CB5 0JX. Telephone: 01638 742065.Email: gingerfold@ukonline.co.uk Website: www.gingerfold.com

Other titles in this series

Typesetting, design and printing by The Burlington Press, Foxton, Cambridge CB2 6SW.

INTRODUCTION

Picture the road haulage scene of fifty years ago. British Road Services was at its peak of operations, although partial de-nationalisation was taking place and many pre-nationalisation hire and reward transport company owners were starting new businesses. BRS operated hundreds of eight-wheelers in its heavy lorry and trunking fleets, and this chassis configuration was popular with numerous own-account hauliers including the major oil and petroleum distributors, flour millers, steel companies, and chemical firms. Leyland Octopus eight-wheelers were top-sellers and were noted for unbeatable reliability and longevity. Many observers would regard the next twenty-five years as a halcyon period for road transport in Great Britain.

Such was the popularity of the Leyland Octopus that its driveline was basically unchanged from 1945 until 1960. Specification options were few in this period, yet the model remained a market leader and waiting lists for new chassis were lengthy. As privately owned road haulage firms re-established themselves in the fifties, it was a Leyland Octopus that was the first choice for many of those whose 'A' Licences allowed heavy lorries.

In my formative years in Lancashire I was surrounded by Leyland Octopus lorries. In addition to aforementioned BRS examples, there were several with operators in and around Bolton. Perhaps the most famous Octopus fleet locally was that of Hipwood and Grundy of Farnworth. They had tankers dedicated to heavy fuel oil and bitumen haulage, and some of these were still running in 1981 when they were at least 25 years old. Latterly they were only used in winter months when demands for boiler fuel were greatest, but these old lorries were there when needed and gave guaranteed reliability.

Something of a local character, Billy Entwistle, drove an Octopus tipper for East Lancashire Paper Mill, collecting coal from local collieries. He always emphasised his steering wheel movements and signalled his left turnings by sticking a painted metal 'hand', attached to a broom handle, through the passenger side window! A couple of L.A.D. cabbed Octopuses were based in Little Lever. Potters chemical works had one, which regularly went to Glasgow, and H.K.R. Transport even owned one. This was the pride and joy of Bill Heap, who would depart each Sunday lunchtime with 20-25 drops of paper for London and the southeast. I once overtook this heavily laden lorry on the M6, and its purring Power-Plus O.680 engine was a delight to hear. It sounded completely on top of its job, as of course it was.

There are many common driveline features between Leyland Octopus models and Leyland Beavers, previously studied in "The Commercial Vehicles Archive Series". It is recommended that *The Leyland Octopus* be read in conjunction with *The Leyland Beaver*. Just as the Beaver range of lorries was highly regarded over the years, then Octopus models carved out an envied reputation for reliability and ruggedness in the most demanding of road transport sectors, when that description was reserved for the heavyweight eight-wheeler market.

Graham Edge, Swaffham Prior, June 2004.

SECTION 1

Leyland Octopus Developments In The 1930s

What an extraordinary period the early 1930s proved to be for the British road transport industry. Not only were commercial vehicles manufacturers forced to appraise and improve their designs, but both freight and passenger services providers were placed under much stricter regulation. This all came about because of the most far-reaching transport legislation ever enacted when the 1933 Road and Rail Traffic Act was passed. This bill and subsequent amendments during the 1930s shaped British transport operations for the next 30 years, until the equally revolutionary statutes of 1964 and 1968.

Whilst some of the 1933 operational legalities for road transport were designed to protect the interests of the Railway Companies, the Construction and Use Regulations demanded a radical rethink from chassis designers. In particular, gross vehicle weights were introduced that required lower unladen weights to maximise legal payloads. It was the end of an era when steam waggons had frequently been ordered from such as Foden and Sentinel. Under the 1933 Traffic Act steam powered vehicles were permitted higher gross weights than internal combustion engined lorries, but there was no payload gain because steamers were considerably heavier. With the compression ignition 'oil' (or diesel) engine gaining rapid acceptance in road vehicles from 1931, heavy and expensive steam waggons were soon deemed to be obsolete.

It was envisaged that after the 1933 parliamentary act British internal combustion engined commercial vehicles would have either two or three axles in rigid format. Maximum gross weights were 12 tons and 19 tons respectively, with various intermediate weight categories. Proportionally, very few articulated lorries were sold, and Scammell of Watford was the main builder of heavyweight artics, and for normal uses these were three axles machines. Drawbar trailers were of course permitted behind rigid lorries, but overall length rules meant that four-wheelers were usually the prime movers.

All the leading manufacturers including Leyland Motors and AEC had introduced new and lighter chassis designs conforming to updated legislation. No doubt fleet engineers and operators, along with chassis designers, assiduously studied these new regulations and one potential loophole was spotted. There was a new 22 tons maximum gross weight category on more than three axles intended for lorry and drawbar trailer combinations. It was therefore reasoned that this could also apply to solo lorries for the simple reason that there was nothing in the Construction and Use Regulations to specifically say that it could not. The difficulty, however, was how to achieve it. A petrol or oil engined six-wheeler had a maximum legal loading of 4 tons on its front axle, and 15 tons across its rear bogie. So the answer was to locate a second front axle behind the first and it only needed a 3 tons load rating. Nor were brakes necessary because the first axle of a drawbar trailer legally could be brakeless. Hence the concept of a rigid eight-wheeler with internal combustion engine evolved.

Credit for this idea is generally attributed to the fleet engineer of the Liverpool Cartage Company, which was a subsidiary company of Thomas Allen. As AEC lorries were their preferred choice, the Southall company assembled the first purpose built, non-steam driven, rigid eight-wheeler in 1934, with unbraked lightweight auxiliary second steering axle. A Mammoth Major six-wheeler chassis was used as the basis for the lorry. And so a chassis configuration that has variously been described as a peculiarity, or British oddity, came into being. Nevertheless the payload advantage of typically 2.5 tons more than a six-wheeler soon ensured the eight-wheeler's enduring popularity for the next 30 years. Other heavy lorry builders soon jumped on the bandwagon and the unbraked second axle concept was adapted by all of them. However, the auxiliary axle was generally given an equal loading tolerance with the first axle.

Apart from the increased payload possible with an eight-wheeler, another consideration that was attractive in the early days of such lorries was a slightly higher legal top speed. Lorries and trailers were restricted to 16 mph, whereas eight-wheelers could travel at 20 mph legally. Also, a second man, or driver's mate, was required for a lorry and trailer, but a rigid eight could carry a similar payload without the additional cost of a second man's wages. Until new eight-wheelers became dedicated designs by mid-1935 or so, several six-wheelers built after 1933 were converted into eight-wheelers. Indeed, this policy continued throughout the 1930s and it was not unusual to see Leyland Hippo six-wheelers, along with similar lorries from other makers, being transformed into eight-wheelers.

The early days of Leyland Motors are briefly described in *The Leyland Beaver*, and by 1934 Leyland regarded itself as the leading designer and producer of premium quality lorries. Most pundits of the time would probably have agreed with that assessment. The company's origin was as a steam waggon builder, which then moved quickly to use internal combustion engines in lorries and passenger vehicles. Conversely, AEC was a later business that never built anything propelled by steam and its first vehicles were motorbuses. Lorries were introduced later, and a fierce rivalry existed between AEC and Leyland as they vied for recognition as market leaders in subsequent years.

No doubt senior management at Leyland was somewhat miffed that AEC had built the first internal combustion engined eight-wheeler, but when the legality of the vehicle was confirmed the Lancashire firm soon had its own design in production. Leyland had developed up to date petrol and diesel engines for its passenger vehicles and heavy lorries such as four-wheeler Beavers and six-wheeler Hippos. Included in the range was an overhead camshaft (ohc) petrol engine of 8.84 litres producing approximately 115 bhp at 2,200 rpm, with 360 lbs. ft. of torque at 1,000 rpm. Alternatively, an ohc compression ignition (diesel) unit of 8.59 litres could be ordered. This was generally referred to as the 8.6 litres C.I. (oil) engine and it produced about 93 bhp at 1,800 to 1,900 rpm with 305 lbs. ft. of torque at 1,300 rpm. Either of these power units could be specified for the new Leyland eight-wheeler, which was given the model name of Octopus. At that time diesel engines were new technology, so until reliability was proven and improved fuel economy became recognised, many operators ordered petrol engines. However, the merits of diesel propulsion had won over most sceptics by the late 1930s and such engines became the usual fitments. Leyland was probably unique in designing its petrol and diesel engines to the same external dimensions, so it was a relatively simple task to replace a thirsty petrol unit with a more frugal diesel in a lorry chassis.

For further details of Leyland pre-war engines refer to *The Leyland Beaver* and Appendix B in this book.

It is probable that the first factory built Leyland eight-wheeler was a converted Hippo, but the company announced its Octopus model in late 1934 or early 1935, and two versions were available. With chassis designation TEW8D, this model had a double drive rear bogie. A trailing fourth axle Octopus was type TEW8T. It is believed that initially just one wheelbase length was offered for this first generation model and it was 16 ft. 10 ins. However, within a few months a longer wheelbase of 18 ft. 10 ins. became available with chassis designations TEW9D, (double drive) and TEW9T, (single drive). These were, in fact, identical wheelbases to contemporary TSW8 and TSW9 Hippo models. See Appendix A for a full listing of Octopus chassis designations.

Depending upon whether a petrol or diesel engine was fitted determined the type of radiator. For the petrol unit vertical "Still" tubes were used, with vertical-gill tubes preferred for the diesel engine. Whichever engine option was specified, then the driveline and chassis details were much the same. A robust single dry plate clutch of 16.25 inches diameter was used. Its pressure plate and facing was designed to allow air to flow through the plate to ensure cooling and long operational life. A clutch stop was fitted to permit clean, quick, gear changes, and the component was fully adjustable for maximum lining wear. Amazingly, this basic clutch size and design was a feature of Leyland heavy lorries, including the Octopus models for more than 30 years, and it was used on Freightline lorries of the 1960s. Only the methods of actuation varied over the years.

The gearbox was in unit construction with the clutch and engine. Comprising four forward speeds and one reverse gear, it was a direct drive top speed design. Of constant mesh design, the gear wheels were helically cut for quieter running. The gearbox casing was cast so that inspection doors could be removed to permit withdrawal of the gears if necessary. There was provision for fitting a mechanically driven tyre pump onto the gearbox and a power take off running at 0.98 engine speed was available as an extra. A three-piece propeller shaft with Spicer couplings transmitted the drive to the rear axles.

A 2-speed auxiliary gearbox could be fitted into the driveline as an optional extra, and this was usually arranged to provide an overdrive ratio for fourth gear only.

The axles in the double drive bogie were fully floating with overhead worm and wheel drives. The worm wheel was carried in adjustable taper-roller races and the hubs were mounted on axle tubes. These also had adjustable taper-roller races. The axle ratio was 8.66:1 and this gave an approximate top speed of 20-25 mph, determined by fitting either a higher revving petrol or lower revving diesel engine. Alternatively, a lower axle ratio of 9.33:1 could be specified, (17-22 mph). Remember, roads were mainly of single carriageway construction in the mid-1930s and heavy lorries were legally confined to a maximum 20 mph speed limit.

If the trailing fourth axle option was ordered then the general rear bogie layout was similar to that of the double drive version. However, the single driving axle was a double reduction design, with first reduction by spiral bevel gears, and second reduction via double helical spur gears. A solid beam trailing axle was used and its hubs and brake drums were fully interchangeable with those fitted to the driven axle. The standard axle ratio was 8.19:1, (22-27 mph) with lower alternative of 9.48:1, (16-21 mph).

Whichever final drive was chosen by the operator then the bogie suspension was the same. It consisted of two inverted semi-elliptic springs with torque rods. These were of tubular assembly with adjustable ball and socket joints provided for each axle. One end of each rod was anchored to an axle casing, with the other extremity fixed to the chassis frame. This arrangement allowed most of the braking and driving torque to be transmitted to the chassis frame and relieved the road springs from excessive stresses.

The chassis frame itself was of quite robust construction, with a deep section. It measured 10.25 inches deep, by 2.5 inches wide, and the steel was three eighths of an inch thick. The steering box was a Marles cam type, and it operated on both front axles by fore and aft drag links. Of course, there was no braking on the second steering axle, but the front axle brake shoes were 3 inches wide and were housed in drums of 17 inches diameter. The rear axles brakes were 6 inches wide in drums of 17 inches diameter. The foot brakes were operated through a master vacuum servo and auxiliary servo by mechanical linkage to the rear shoes. Front wheel braking was by separate auxiliary servos mounted directly onto the axle arms. Actuation was by a control valve on the master servo unit. The hand brake for parking purposes was a multi-push lever working a mechanical loose-link pick-up onto each individual brake shoe.

Standard sized tyres were provided on each axle and were 36" x 8"; singles on the front axles and twin wheels on the rear. Ten stud fixing wheels were fitted. Some operators did specify larger single wheels on the back axles with "balloon" tyres.

A large capacity fuel tank was provided for either engine choice and it held 55 gallons. Fuel feed to the engine carburettor, or diesel injection pump, depending on the unit fitted, was by gravity from a two gallons capacity autovac.

As was common practice with premium quality commercial vehicles builders in those days, chassis lubrication was by grouped Tecalamit grease nipples placed in easily accessible positions.

Petrol engined Octopus chassis were provided with a 12-volt electrical system, but there was no starter motor as standard. One was available as an extra, but a driver was expected to start the big petrol engine with a starting handle. The diesel powered Octopus also had 12-volt lighting, but there was a 24-volt starter motor provided. This was operated by a foot switch.

As Leyland Motors also had a large body building division it would supply its Octopus as a complete vehicle with coach built cab and either a flat platform, or dropsided body. Or, it would supply the vehicle as just a chassis and front scuttle for the purchaser to equip with cab and body of his choice. A third option was to order as a chassis with coach built cab. If the complete lorry was bought then Leyland offered a choice of varnish finished paint schemes in four standard colours, namely green, blue, red, or grey. A "reasonable" amount of sign writing and lining out was included in the price.

Early Leyland Octopus lorries were designed for operating at 22 tons gross weight. This was also the maximum gross train weight for a lorry and drawbar trailer of the time, so an eight-wheeler could not pull a trailer. Moreover, a prime mover could not be more than 26 feet long, so Octopuses were also disqualified for that reason. A typical unladen weight for a TEW8D Octopus with petrol engine, Leyland built cab and flat platform, was 7 tons, allowing a legal payload of 15 tons. A similar diesel engined Octopus was 5 cwts heavier, giving 14.75 tons payload. Trailing axle TEW8T Octopuses were correspondingly 3 cwts lighter, permitting even better payloads.

These were highly commendable tare weights and payloads and Leyland had succeeded in building a relatively light eight-wheeler at its first attempt. The Octopus was almost a ton lighter than the competing AEC Mammoth Major eight-wheeler, forcing AEC to re-design and lighten its model within a few months of being first in the field. Almost from the beginning of eight-wheeler production Leyland assumed market-leading status with its Octopus model, a position it was to protect jealously for the next twenty-five years.

Nevertheless, after a couple of years of production Leyland Motors decided to revise the specification of its Octopus eight-wheelers. New chassis references were introduced in 1937 and these signified a stronger chassis frame. Weight saving measures were taken with other components, and especially so with the rear bogies and suspension arrangements. The trailing axle variant received a lightened, 4-spring rear suspension. The nett effect was slightly lighter vehicles than previously, and on average legal payloads were better by a couple of hundredweights.

These new type designations were TEW11, which was a double drive bogie, 15 ft. 10 ins. wheelbase lorry. TEW12 signified the same rear axles but on a 17 ft. 10 ins. wheelbase. The trailing axle models were TEW14T and TEW15T on 15 ft. 11 ins. and 17 ft. 11 ins. wheelbases respectively. The frame depth on the double drive models was extended by a couple of inches to 12 inches, and thicker steel of five sixteenth of one inch was used. Trailing axle variants had frames marginally thinner at 0.25 inch thickness, and fractionally less deep. Short wheelbase chassis were equipped with smaller 44 gallons capacity fuel tanks.

Octopus engine options were unchanged and the clutch for diesel versions received a flexible centre. Once again, this feature remained for many years to come. However, there were significant changes with the transmission and the auxiliary 2-speed gearbox was discontinued. Instead purchasers were given the option of either a 5-speed close ratio unit with direct drive top speed, or a 5-speed gearbox with overdrive top ratio. Both were constant mesh designs, but first and second gears were machined with straight spur teeth, and the remaining gears were single helicals engaged by sliding dogs. If the overdrive gearbox was fitted top speeds were increased by approximately 6 mph, if compared with corresponding earlier models. Rear axle ratios remained as before.

The rear axles options were also as for the first Octopuses, but suspensions were improved. For the double drive bogie there was now a central pivot 2-spring inverted semi-elliptic system with torque rods. A revised layout locating each spring as high as possible relative to the chassis frame gave more stability and better articulation, which in turn resulted in greater adhesion on rough surfaces and ensured that under normal conditions drive could not be lost. The trailing axle bogie suspension was completely new and was a 4-spring semi-elliptical design with the springs anchored to the chassis at their outer ends. The inner ends were shackled to the frame through a rocking bar attachment. This was a considerably lighter arrangement than the 2-spring suspension.

Braking, steering, and electrical systems were identical to TEW8 models.

In the year 1938 there were further amendments to the Octopus specification. Some were minor changes, such as a mechanical fuel pump being fitted to petrol versions in place of an autovac. The 8.6 litres C.I. (oil) engine was re-tuned for a worthwhile increase in power, its new rating becoming 106 bhp at 1,900 rpm and 330 lbs. ft. of torque at 1,200 rpm.

Interestingly, the 5-speed overdrive gearbox option was discontinued with the only choice becoming a 5-speed direct drive unit. Rear axle ratios were revised to provide similar overall gearing and top speeds to the overdrive gearbox. Double drive axles ratios were standardised at 7.33:1, with optional lower gearing of 8.66:1, and the single drive bogie axle was slightly higher geared at 7.15:1. A lower ratio of 8.19:1 could be ordered if thought necessary. Significantly, the inverted 2-spring double drive bogie suspension was replaced by the same 4-spring arrangement used for trailing axle 8 x 2 chassis as a weight saving measure. Finally, chassis designations were amended; model TEW11 became TEW14D with TEW12 changing to TEW15D to identify chassis with new rear suspensions.

Advertised prices for leading eight-wheelers in 1939 make interesting comparisons. A Leyland Octopus with diesel engine and in chassis / front scuttle guise was quoted at £1,815. An AEC Mammoth Major Mk.II rigid eight in identical format was £1,825, and a Foden DG eight-wheeler chassis with Gardner 6LW engine was a surprising £1,710. These prices confirm the premium quality lorries built by Leyland Motors

In the 5 years that elapsed between eight-wheeler lorries appearing on British roads and the outbreak of the Second World War all the domestic heavy commercial vehicles builders had entered the market. Sales of these "kings of the roads" were important and Leyland Motors with its Octopus range was recognised as being one of the leading designers and manufacturers of the type. An Octopus could carry a satisfactory legal payload economically and reliably and the model was a firm favourite with numerous operators. The 1939-45 war ended any further chassis developments until peace returned, as Leyland Motors concentrated its huge manufacturing resources on the war effort. Nevertheless, pre-war Octopus lorries had vital and important roles to fulfil, transporting all kinds of goods and war materials throughout the country.

One of the early Leyland Octopus chassis, and probably the very first one, that was converted from a Hippo six-wheeler chassis by the works. The photo was taken in 1935 with the lorry being on single balloon tyres on its rear axles. It was used as a demonstrator to prospective customers.

An early dropside bodied Octopus that entered service with Latham & Son, of Ratby, Leicester, in 1935. This was also supplied with single rear wheels, a policy that seemed to be favoured by Leyland Motors with its heavy lorries in those days. Note the lack of "Octopus" badge; could it be that the model name had not been decided for these first Leyland eight-wheelers?

More conventional in appearance with twin rear wheels, fleet number 22 with James Bridge (St.Helens) Ltd. The lorry was on contract to Forster's Glass, a local company. The lorry had an unladen weight of a shade less than 7 tons, allowing a legal payload of 15 tons.

Motor Carriers (Liverpool) Ltd. bought three Leyland Octopuses in 1935, and this one had an unladen weight of 6 tons 17 cwts. Plenty of information about the company was portrayed on the cab.

Ingham & Tipping from Bamber Bridge enjoyed a very long relationship with its local lorry producer, and this large animal foods miller bought one of the early Octopus chassis in 1935. It was fitted with a bulk body for carrying grain that was discharged by gravity either through the floor or by a side chute.

Large flour miller Hovis was another long established Leyland customer and bought this Octopus at a time when it was still running steam wagons in 1935. Hovis had one of the most understated liveries of any miller.

Early Octopus TEW tippers were extremely rare, so this photograph of an unregistered and unlettered tipper from 1936 is an important find. The substantial wooden body was hoisted by under floor hydraulic powered tipping gear, and remember this was at a time when some loads were still shovelled on and off by hand, so this must have been regarded as an advanced lorry then. The records show a company named Hampton, who specified that the fuel tank be positioned behind the cab, bought it.

Loading sand with a Ruston Bucyrus excavator for construction of the Formby by-pass in 1938. The Octopus was owned by Woodward's of Formby, haulage contractors and sand and gravel merchants. Woodward's were also main Leyland Motors agents in west and south Lancashire.

An interesting pre-WWII street scene with the Octopus of Kinders Garage and Haulage Ltd., Blaby, Leicester, centre stage. Its load comprised a couple of large Ransomes cement mixers. Kinders were managed by the redoubtable and famous Miss A.M. ('Ma') Walker who was known for reducing many a tough lorry driver to a quivering wreck!

The overhead crane with its massive hook was loading sheet steel at Baldwins Ltd., Wilden Ironworks, Stourport. Apparently slings were not used for lifting the bales of steel. By 1937 when the photo was taken, Baldwins had at least a couple of Leyland eight-wheelers in service.

A beautifully liveried Octopus of Taylor Walker, the Limehouse, east London, brewer, loading crates of bottles by hand. The lorry's body was made by Lamboll in typical brewer's dray style. Also evident are different modes of transport, namely a hand truck, a horse cart, and of course a much older Leyland lorry.

This was a scene in 1937 with Cadbury's famous Bournville factory being extended. Gupwell of Birmingham bought three Octopuses in that year, with trailing fourth axles. The van on the left of the picture was from Cadbury's Sound Film Unit.

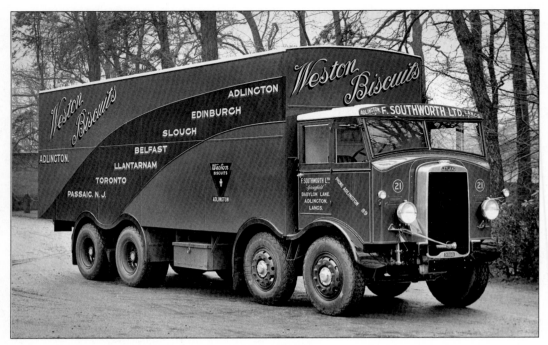

Canadian entrepreneur, Garfield Weston, was building his empire in the late 1930s by acquiring bread bakeries and biscuit factories. F. Southworth Ltd. of Adlington, Chorley, was contracted for storage and distribution of Weston Biscuits, and this Octopus van, new in 1939, was kept busy collecting up to three loads of biscuits weekly from Edinburgh, Slough, or South Wales for the warehouse at Adlington.

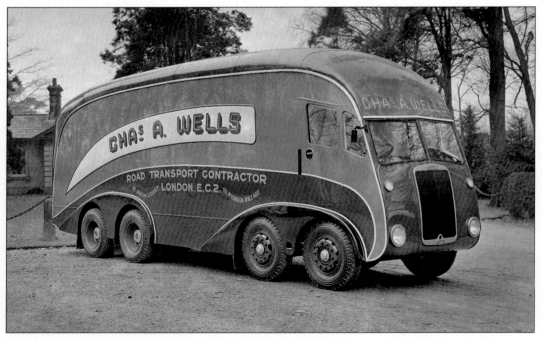

Even as long ago as 1939 some bodybuilders attempted to implement streamlined designs. Looking quite advanced for its time, this Octopus van was about to enter service with Chas. A. Wells of London on long distance road haulage services.

Leyland Motors' contribution to the war effort between 1939-45 is well documented and it was also an important manufacturer of battle tanks. A few special 10 x 4 Octopus lorries were constructed with strengthened chassis and body cross-members for transporting medium tanks a few miles from the works to the railway station. There they were loaded onto flatbed railcars for onward transportation.

Bowler & Mack specialised in moving theatrical scenery as well as more mundane general haulage work. One Sunday morning in 1949 this elderly Octopus TEW was used for moving the set of an "Old Mother Riley" production from the New Cross Empire into storage. The front tyres of the Leyland were virtually bald and it was missing its offside headlamp. "Old Mother Riley" was a comedy caricature of a fictional Irish washerwoman, portrayed by Arthur Lucan. Kitty McShane, Lucan's wife in real life, played 'her' stage daughter.

R. Kirk & Sons of Nottingham was still running this 1937 Octopus thirteen years later in 1950, when it was used for hauling an overhead crane gantry from Royce Cranes of Loughborough to Middlesborough. The load was 74 feet long and a rear dolly had to be used.

Kirk's also operated a very early Octopus, supplied in 1935, and this was the lorry when almost new engaged on another abnormal loads movement, comprising a gantry for an overhead crane.

SECTION 2
Post-War Octopus Models

For more details of Leyland Motors' wartime production, including important engine developments, please refer to *The Leyland Beaver.* Another book in "The Commercial Vehicles Archive Series", titled *The Leyland Comet,* also provides background information about production difficulties in the post-war years caused by raw materials shortages.

By 1945 it became apparent that an Allied Forces victory was inevitable, so management at Leyland was able to start planning its post-war business strategy with some certainty. The priority was for commercial and passenger vehicles of all kinds to replace pre-war models that at best were worn out because of continuous usage, or, at worst, obsolete. In late 1945 Leyland announced its ranges of buses, coaches, and lorries for peacetime, with production planned to start as soon as possible when factories had reverted to normal working.

To begin with the new Leyland post-war catalogue was fairly limited and consisted of modernised pre-war best sellers. These incorporated technological advances resulting from wartime developments, with the O.600 diesel engine being a prime example. Some models were an amalgam of earlier design features and latest ideas, and the new Octopus eight-wheeler fitted this description.

Whilst the Leyland Octopus was listed for availability in 1945 it is doubtful if any, other than prototypes, were actually built until 1946. A different, numerical, chassis identification system was used and for lorries the first number signified their gross vehicle weights. Accordingly, "22" was 22 tons and represented the top weight Octopus. There were only two versions; 22.O/1 was a 17 ft. 9 ins. wheelbase haulage chassis with 22.O/3 being a 15 ft. 6 ins. tipper lorry. Tare weights were somewhat heavier than pre-war models, and typically the longer Octopus with a 24 ft. 6 ins. long wooden flat platform body weighed 7.5 tons, permitting a legal payload of 14.5 tons. The shorter variant provided 18 ft. 6 ins. of body space, and with an aluminium alloy tipping body the Octopus was approximately 8.5 tons empty for a legal 13.5 tons payload. However, Octopuses were ruggedly constructed, - the chassis dimensions and thickness was identical to 1938 frame specification, - and some measure of overloading was common in those days with many operators.

Numerous purchasers tested the strength of new Octopus lorries in another way. In 1942 as a wartime measure to fully utilise available resources, the 26 feet length limitation for a drawbar trailer prime mover was rescinded to permit eight-wheelers to pull trailers. The maximum gross train weight for such an outfit was raised to 30 tons and after the war ended this status-quo remained, so the evocative sight of an 'eight-wheeler and drag' became legal.

Power for a post-war Leyland Octopus lorry was provided by a new 9.8 litres capacity diesel engine that had been developed during the war. Designated O.600, (O = oil, 600 = approximate engine capacity in cubic inches), this unit produced 125 bhp at 1,800 rpm, with 410 lbs. ft. of torque at 900 rpm. A Simms injection pump with Leyland multi-hole injectors was used for the fuel system and a "Still" tube radiator was fitted. For further details about this acclaimed engine see *The Leyland Beaver* and Appendix B in this book.

A 5-speed direct top gearbox was in unit construction with the clutch and engine and this had provision for either full power, or 10 horsepower ptos. The clutch was identical to that used on earlier Octopuses.

Whereas pre-war Leyland eight-wheelers had offered prospective buyers a choice of double or single drive rear bogies, the post-war versions were standardised with only double drive being available. No doubt this was determined by the production constraints placed on the company during this period and the need for manufacturing to its optimum capacity during a difficult time. Also, the government was demanding that export quotas should be met, although eight-wheelers were mainly destined for the home market.

For the double drive rear axles overhead wheel and worm drive was retained. Ratios were 7:33:1 (standard), with optional gearings of 6:5:1, 8.66:1, and 9.33:1. An Octopus with the standard ratio could reach a top speed of about 28 mph, although the 20 mph limit still applied. The modernised bogie suspension was similar in principle to the pre-war offering, it being a 2-spring inverted semi-elliptic system. The outer ends of the springs were attached to the axles by swivelling trunnions and torque rods were located from the axles casings to the chassis frame. This was a tough suspension and rarely gave problems.

Steering also followed earlier practise with a Marles cam and double roller steering box. Once again, in accepted tradition, the second steering axle was unbraked. A new braking system was used and this was a two leading shoe, wedge operated, vacuum servo-assisted hydraulic set-up. Front axle brake shoes were 3 inches wide, and those on the rear wheels were 5 inches wide. All brake drums were 16.25 inches diameter. The total braking area for the lorry was 827 square inches, and a pull-on mechanical handbrake operated on the rear wheels only, providing 636 square inches of parking brake.

Early post-war Octopuses were shod with 36" x 8" tyres on ten stud wheels, but these were superseded by 9.00 x 20, 12 ply covers. A 55 gallons fuel tank was standard on the long wheelbase chassis, and a 44 gallons tank was provided for the tipper lorry. Chassis lubrication was similar to pre-war models and a 24-volt electrical system was fitted.

One major difference was immediately apparent on new Octopuses. Whereas pre-war lorries had coach built cabs, from 1946 Leyland built all-metal cabs were provided. This design was plain and simple, with flat metal panels being mainly used in construction. But the end result was not unattractive. Early cabs had no exterior embellishments, but as rationing and shortages eased, later versions received some bright metal trimmings. The radiator was enclosed behind a mesh grille.

Very few options were listed for '22' series Octopuses. They were totally standardised lorries, reflecting the austere conditions of the time. Apart from a gearbox driven tyre pump, any options were mainly associated with drawbar trailer duties, including a spring-loaded pin and jaw, and trailer brakes operating gear. This could be either hand operated by the statutory second man, (or driver's mate), or a vacuum connection if the trailer was equipped with vacuum operated brakes.

One important option that did become available from 1951 was the new Leyland O.680 engine of 11.1 litres capacity, or 680 cubic inches. It was developed from the O.600 unit in response to demands for more power from overseas customers of Leyland Motors. This power unit produced 150 bhp at 2,000 rpm, with 450 lbs. ft. of torque at 1,100 rpm and it was a popular choice with Octopus operators that regularly pulled drawbar trailers.

In spite of the standard, even basic, specification offered to Octopus purchasers, the model continued to sell very well. In particular, British Road Services, which enjoyed a virtual monopoly of road haulage between 1948 and 1953, was a good customer for Octopuses. Plenty of own account hauliers also ordered in quantity.

By the year 1954 Leyland Motors was able to update some of its models. In part this was dictated by customer demands and also by significant, imminent, changes to road transport legislation. British Road Services was in the process of being partially de-nationalised, resulting in the re-emergence of a competing, privately funded road haulage industry. A long-awaited increase in lorry gross vehicle weights was due for implementation in 1955, and although it was a modest increment of 2 tons, it allowed solo eight-wheelers to legally run at 24 tons, and those pulling drawbar trailers to gross 32 tons. To provide a margin of tolerance for heavier loads, 9.00 x 24, 12 ply tyres could be fitted to special order.

For 1955 revised Octopus specifications were issued, with new chassis designations. These were 24.O/4 for the long wheelbase version, which retained the same axles spacing as before, and 24.O/5 for the tipper variant, again with the same wheelbase as previously. Tare weights were slightly higher because heavier cabs and braking components were fitted. The load carrier could typically carry about 16.25 tons of payload within the 24 tons gross weight limit. If a trailer was pulled this usually added between 6 and 7 tons. The Octopus tipper was good for a load of about 15.5 tons, depending on the construction of the body.

The main features of '24' series Octopuses were their modernised cabs and full air pressure braking systems. Engine choices remained the same, either an O.600, or O.680. By now a C.A.V. fuel injection pump was usually fitted, with Leyland four-hole injectors.

Many components were as before, including clutch, gearbox, rear axles and bogie suspension. A trailing fourth axle option was offered once more, after an absence of some 16 years. However, it is believed that no more than forty Octopuses were built with this particular feature, which is surprising because the majority of British haulage contractors favoured trailing axle configurations for six and eight-wheelers engaged on general haulage traffic. This was, of course, to reduce tare weights and maximise payloads.

The driveline offered a new optional choice. It was an auxiliary gearbox of 1.328:1 ratio that could be arranged as either a step-up (overdrive), or a step-down (reduction) feature. As an overdrive it gave such an Octopus a top speed of about 35 mph, and in reduction mode it was a useful means of improving the hill climbing performance of a lorry pulling a trailer.

For heavier gross weights Leyland switched to full air pressure braking using cam operated internal expanding brake shoes. Compared with their predecessors, new Octopuses had bigger brakes as well. Front axle brake shoes were now 4 inches wide, with those on the back wheels being 6 inches wide. Drums of 16.75 inches diameter were fitted to the three braked axles. The total footbrake area was 916 square inches, with a parking brake area of 682 square inches. A multi-pull ratchet type mechanical handbrake operated on the rear wheels only. If the Octopus was engaged on drawbar trailer work the trailer brakes could be either air, or hand operated by the second man. Because many vacuum braked trailers were still used, air-braked Octopus could be specified with an exhauster compressor with breakaway valves for operating trailer brakes.

In the year 1954 Leyland modernised its heavy lorry cabs. All-metal fabrication was retained, but new drivers' structures were now double skinned and insulated. A wider panel with bright metal, 'Birmabright,' horizontal louvres, replaced the mesh grille. A more comfortable and improved interior was provided for driver and mate, including the previously unprecedented luxury of heater and windscreen de-mister. Some of the last vacuum-hydraulic braked Octopuses received the new Leyland cab, and it was fitted to all air-braked versions. Quite a few older lorries were re-cabbed with the new structure in later years when chassis were re-furbished for further service. Remember, in the 1950s a premium quality vehicle such as an Octopus was designed for a minimum ten years service life, with fifteen years being required and expected by some hauliers.

During the fifteen years or so that '22' and '24' series Leyland Octopus chassis were in production sales levels were consistent. Whilst options were few throughout this period it coincided with a time when the average British transport boss was happy to take what was on offer from manufacturers, provided their offerings were reliable and gave lengthy service lives. However, by the end of the 1950s a certain era was drawing to a close and purchasers were becoming more demanding.

An early '22' series Octopus photographed in 1947. At this time, and for a couple of years, cabs were unadorned, with no bright metal embellishments, and consequently rather plain. Blunt Bros.' bought the chassis and cab from Arlington Motors and fitted the body themselves after removing it from a 1934 Leyland Hippo they had scrapped. In those austere post-war years when food was rationed the Octopus was working under the auspices of Meat Transport Organisation Ltd., (M.T.O.L.)

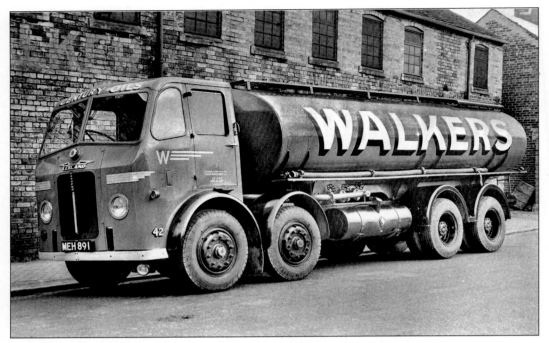

The Octopus chassis became a favourite with tanker operators and this Butterfields tank had a capacity of 3,500 gallons. In 1949 this Leyland was regularly hauling lubricating oil from Walkers' refinery at Hanley to Ellesmere Port and Liverpool.

Petrofina of Belgium established itself in Great Britain in 1939, buying Cities Service Oil Company. In 1948 Fina, as it was generally known, started to expand rapidly and acquired a fleet of eight-wheeler tankers. Leyland became the predominant make in its heavyweight tanker category. This six-compartment Octopus spirit tanker was based at Fina's depot on Preston Docks. Fina is now part of the Total Oil Company.

Bournville in Birmingham is famous as the home of Cadbury's chocolate, but the raw materials of cocoa, sugar, and milk are blended to make chocolate crumb at Marlbrook, near Leominster. This was the busy scene there in 1951 with a partly hidden Bedford O type unloading milk churns in the background, and an Octopus '22' series tanker used for bulk collections from other supplying creameries.

A very common sight in the era of the '22' series Octopus was a load of packing cases bound for the docks. In 1949 William Asquith Ltd. of Halifax won a large order for supplying machine tools to a customer in Sydney, and this impressive consignment was bound for Liverpool Docks. The vacuum reservoir can be prominently seen on the Octopus chassis.

BRS was the biggest purchaser of '22' series Octopuses and by 1950, the date of this photo, they were appearing in quantity with the state owned haulier. This one was based at Stockport depot and was destined for a dock with its huge packing case, which probably contained a Mirlees Blackstone industrial or marine diesel engine. The background warehouses and ornate bridge ironwork paint a nostalgic picture of over 50 years ago.

Gosnell Bros. Ltd. of Bermondsey, southeast London used this Octopus and trailer for carrying sawn timber to the Midlands car plants where it was made into packing cases for exporting components. The lorry was new in 1954 and it had the more powerful O.680 engine option plus an auxiliary 2-speed step-up gearbox. Note the apparently haphazard means of loading the stacks of timber with only three restraining and securing chains. High loads of timber were notorious for slipping.

An Octopus that was based in the northwestern Highlands of Scotland. To assist in regenerating that remote area, the Duke of Westminster Estates Company bought Sutherland Transport and Trading Co. Ltd. of Lairg as a means of providing its tenants and crofters with readily available transport for their goods. Outgoing loads usually comprised timber, fish, and livestock with back loads being animal feedstuffs, fertilizer and agricultural machinery.

This was the old Covent Garden Market in its heyday of the mid-fifties. Hustle, bustle, and frantic activity with porters pushing handbarrows and drivers loading lorries. A couple of the Octopuses were London based, but the centre lorry was from South Wales and after a trunking duty was re-loading fruit and vegetables for its home region.

A huge block of granite causing plenty of interest at Aberdeen Railway station. The locally quarried rock had been carried by an Aberdeen based '22' series Octopus and the thickness of the slinging wire ropes suggest that the weight of the load could have exceeded legal limits. If so, special authority would have been granted to move it a few miles by road for onward transportation by rail.

The famous crane maker, Herbert Morris of Loughborough, specialised in overhead factory crane installations and this movement in 1951 was one of two bridge girders for a 50 tons capacity overhead crane. The girder weighed 13 tons and was 76 feet long. A very awkward load with an extremely high centre of gravity for the Octopus driver to handle.

Structural engineers Redpath, Brown & Co. Ltd. also had plenty of over length loads to move and these steel girders were supported on heavy-duty bolsters. The location was the Tower of London with a rare Commer six-wheeler also in the shot.

C. Bristow Ltd. was a subsidiary within the famous Davis Bros. group and their Octopus had loaded alum at Peter Spence (Chemicals) Widnes in 1957. The load was destined for one of the paper mills of Thames Board. Note the rolled sheet in the roof box.

Two Octopuses belonging to Dawson Bros. Ltd. of Cleckheaton and Wanstead about to set off for Tennants Wellpark Brewery in Duke Street, Glasgow, with what at the time would become the biggest bottle washer in Scotland. The small driver's mirror was totally ineffectual for such loads and cloth rags were used until proper marker boards became available in later years.

The scene was Gladstone Dock, Liverpool, in 1958 with a locally based Octopus of BRS waiting in the queue. There is plenty of history contained in this picture; a couple of Hanson's AECs, and another AEC Mammoth Major belonging to J.C. Ashworth of Bradford. Oh, and also a Mersey Docks and Harbour Board shunting engine. Such scenes can never be repeated.

Today, Biffa is one of the leading waste disposal companies, but as Richard Biffa Ltd. the company was also involved in 'muck away' tipper haulage. In 1959 these Octopuses were some five years old, but still with years of life in them. They were being loaded with clay by a Ruston Bucyrus 22RB at Hither Green, southeast London, where new railway sheds were being built by Taylor Woodrow. With 14 cu. yd. bodies on the Octopuses they could also transport domestic waste to landfill sites.

By 1955 '24' series Octopuses were entering service, with full air brakes and restyled cabs. E.E. Bamford (Contractors) Ltd. of Alfreton was an early purchaser of these popular eight-wheelers, but there are a couple of fascinating aspects to this picture of an otherwise traditional British general haulage lorry. "Spaceships" were figments of imagination in 1955, and the final digit on the number plate appears to have been pressed out the wrong way round.

This was the scene in 1955 at Hollins Paper Mill, Darwen, with wallpaper base paper being loaded onto a new Octopus. The reels were delivered to associate companies in Lancashire and Yorkshire where they were converted into wall coverings. Return loads were either waste paper or pulp. The loading bay canopy would not provide wet weather protection, as lorries had got progressively longer. Note the old Leyland Beaver in shot, then twenty years old and still going strong. It still is, albeit in preservation.

This was a well-stacked load of imported potatoes on Chas. Riddle's '24' series Octopus. The operator was a South Wales based potato merchants.

The well-remembered Trafford Park firm of Bannister, Walton & Co. Ltd. had a good load of steel girders on its Octopus in 1955. Note the substantial flat platform body with sturdy, reinforced supporting bolsters for the longer sections.

Based at Morley, Leeds, Bulk Liquid Transport Limited's brand new and unregistered Octopus tanker. The spare wheel was in an unusual location for a long wheelbase tanker. The company was a subsidiary of Peter Slater Ltd., tipper haulier.

General Refractories Ltd. was a committed Leyland operator. This short wheelbase Octopus 24.O/5 tipper entered service in 1957 and it was used for carrying foundry sand.

In more recent times Gibbs of Fraserburgh was known for its smart fleet of refrigerated vehicles until the closure of the firm a couple of years ago. Back in the days when it was a general haulier it used an Octopus from its base in northeast Scotland on long distance work. Note the 'AA' badge on the cab. The load appeared to be coils of wire rope and the outer ones were canted inwards on the side rave for improved stability.

Sheffield based Cooper & Hart Ltd. had a typical steel hauliers low dropside body on its Octopus in 1958, although it was being loaded with pallets of carbon electrodes in this instance. The forklift truck driver had the pallet a long way from the mast; not in the best interests of safety and today would bring a reprimand from a Health & Safety Officer.

Named "Diana" of The Long Haul, Leyland Motors Works Transport Octopus was back on more mundane duties in 1958, loading export components for Calcutta. The lorry had recently featured prominently in a well-remembered film starring British actress Diana Dors, and American leading man Victor Mature. After serving in the works fleet the lorry was bought by a haulage contractor, but it was later destroyed by fire.

The 1950s saw the introduction of bulk carrying and discharge bodies for powders and granular products. ICI used several Octopuses with twin 7-ton capacity containers for carrying salt in bulk to food processing factories, tanneries, and other chemicals producers.

Apparently this was a re-cabbed '22' series vacuum-hydraulic braked Octopus, quite a common policy by operators wanting to present an up-to date image. W.A. North & Son Ltd. of Bourne, Lincolnshire ran frequently with straw to The Straw Pulp Manufacturing Co. at Mount Sion Works, Radcliffe. There the straw was processed into pulp for papermaking. The lorry was equipped with a hydraulic Telehoist side-loader. The twin-wheeled trailer was usually 'piggy-backed' home.

Typical Octopus wagon and drag outfit of the fifties, which was on contract from Road Services (Caledonian) at Dumfries depot. The main load was chipboard, probably from Annan factory, with a few steel drums on top for good measure.

The diversity of loads carried by eight-wheelers was truly wondrous. Well known Gloucestershire haulier George Read (Transport) Ltd. was testing its Octopus with an excavator's jib and bucket. The machine's tracks were also on the lorry, but the blocks of wood supporting the jib over the back axles looked none too secure.

Around 1960 better methods of handling bulky materials such as domestic waste were being introduced, with Dempster Dumpmaster hydraulic compacting bodies, such as this, becoming popular. Fowler & Froud Ltd. of Mitcham placed this late '24' series Octopus in service in 1962.

Peter Slater Ltd. was one of the success stories of the 1950s. The owner founded it when he was just 21 on leaving the Army in 1946. He used his gratuity to buy his first lorry. By 1953 he had twenty-four eight-wheeler tippers in service, running from the Yorkshire and Nottinghamshire coalfields to the northwest and Lancashire. The lorries were all double shifted, doing four loads in a twenty-four hours period. Drivers were reputedly on bonus schemes, but they also received sick pay and had a superannuation scheme, very unusual then. The 'greedy boards' on this Octopus were typical of coal haulage in 1960.

The family firm of Hinchliffe based at Walmersley, Bury, dated back to well before the Second World War and only went out of the haulage business in recent years. It was noted for its exceptionally smart lorries. Here an Octopus was loading pulp at Preston Docks, which handled large tonnages from Scandinavia destined for the Lancashire paper mills, of which there were several around Bury and Radcliffe. Local haulage companies involved in pulp haulage expected at least two round trips daily from drivers.

Manchester Tankers Ltd. was an associate company of Oswald Kay Transport. The tank-cleaning offshoot specialised in collecting and disposing of unwanted by-products remaining from processes using petroleum products for manufacturing plastics. These were regularly pumped into disused mineshafts, of which there was an abundance in the Tyldesley, Walkden, and Little Hulton districts, west of Manchester. These residues were highly inflammable and toxic. A magnetic probe in the tank wired to a control box in the Octopus cab showed the volume of the load.

An imposing sight as a couple of Octopuses of Staveley's manoeuvred their abnormal loads round a sharp bend in 1966. The leading '24' series was followed by a newer L.A.D. type. The fabrications were hatch covers for a ship and were 54 feet long by 16 feet wide and each weighed 18 tons. As these outfits qualified as lorry and trailer combinations they were running legally within the 32 tons gross train weight limit. The destination was Belfast.

SECTION 3

Power-Plus Octopus Range

Times were changing by 1960. Road haulage was a buoyant business as freight traffic was steadily won from the railways. In the year 1958 the Preston By-pass was opened to gain the distinction of being the first Motorway graded road in Great Britain. Shortly afterwards, a much longer stretch of the M1 opened in the Midlands. The Motorway age had dawned, co-incidentally with several of the old trunk routes being re-built into dual carriageways and some of the bottleneck towns being by-passed. Also, the 20 mph speed limit for heavy lorries was abolished in 1957, so the potential for quicker journey times was being created. But only if lorries were capable of higher speeds and to attain them required more power and extra gears. Faster running also demanded improved brakes. The lumbering Octopus of 28 mph flat out was rapidly becoming outmoded for both long distance haulage and inter-city trunking duties. Rugged and reliable as the post-war designs were a new model was needed.

There were also discernible changes in buying patterns for heavy vehicles at this time. From being the undoubted flagship lorries of transport fleets, the 'kings of the road' eight-wheelers were slowly being usurped by articulated lorries. So, in September 1960 Leyland Motors announced its heavyweight Power-Plus ranges. This was not just a modernisation of existing models, but also a wholesale re-design of chassis, drivelines, and cabs.

The Octopus model name had become synonymous with Leyland eight-wheelers, so it was retained for the new Power-Plus models, which were fitted with Vista Vue L.A.D. cabs. See *The Leyland Beaver* for further details. There were no increases in gross vehicle weights at this time, but two haulage Octopus models were announced with non-reactive rear suspensions on wheelbases of 17 feet 0 inches and 14 feet 9 inches. Alternatively these chassis could be specified with what was described as rigid rear bogies. A tipper version on a 14 feet 9 inches wheelbase was only available with a rigid bogie. Chassis designations were far more complex and are listed in Appendix A.

The non-reactive rear suspension was about 10 cwts lighter than a rigid bogie chassis, and was designed for high-speed trunk roads and Motorways running. Typically, a long wheelbase Octopus with this suspension, and aluminium alloy and wooden flat platform body, tared off at approximately 8 tons, giving a payload of 16 tons. This lighter springing arrangement comprised a non-reactive bell crank lever, 4-spring suspension. The front ends of the springs were anchored to the chassis frame and the rear of each spring was fixed to bell crank rocking levers, which in turn were connected by means of tie rods. These tie rods were not subjected to bending stresses, so the load was distributed equally between the axles. Consequently, braking torque was fully compensated and loss of traction caused by axle hop during unladen emergency braking applications was prevented.

The alternative rigid bogie suspension was for heavy-duty work in this country and it was standard for Octopus chassis being exported. Basically, it was the same inverted 2-spring system with torque rods used since 1946. However, for both rigid and non-reactive suspensions long, easy riding, high deflection semi-elliptic springs were used. Both front axles springs were assisted by shock absorbers. The first axle was set back, or retracted, on these new Octopuses.

Whichever rear bogie was chosen caused newly developed driving axles to be used. The long serving worm and wheel components were declared obsolete, to be replaced by double drive, spiral bevel axles with secondary epicyclic hub reduction and lockable third differential. The standard overall ratio was 6.06:1, with options of 7.74:1 or 4.82:1. The top speed of a Power-Plus Octopus was decided by the gearbox fitted, but if it were a 6-speed overdrive type, then 55 mph was possible with the highest axle option. For the home market only, a trailing fourth axle with non-reactive suspension could be specified, but with limitations on its duties. Such an Octopus should not have been used for drawbar trailer work and it had just an O.600 engine with either a 5 or 6-speed gearbox. There was a useful further saving of 9 cwts in unladen weight with this particular eight-wheeler specification.

Development of Power-Plus engines is adequately covered in *The Leyland Beaver*, with further information available in Appendix B. New Octopuses were equipped with a standard power unit and this was the Power-Plus O.600 engine. Described as the "super economy" version, this re-tuned O.600 produced 140 bhp at 1,700 rpm, with 438 lbs. ft. of torque at 1,200 rpm. Alternatively, customers could order Octopuses with O.680 engines that now produced 200 bhp at 2,200 rpm and 548 lbs. ft. of torque at 1,200 rpm. Such units were standard in Octopus eight-wheelers destined for overseas clients.

A 'no loss' cooling system was used for these new engines, based on a 4-row Morris type stack radiator. There was a separate receiving container for collecting any coolant expelled from the header tank via the overflow pipe. When the engine cooled, the liquid was siphoned into the radiator.

Not surprisingly the long-serving clutch was retained unchanged, but new, stronger gearboxes were fitted. They were designed to cope with higher torque produced by Power-Plus engines. All were constant mesh units and those available were a 5-speed direct top gearbox, a 6-speed overdrive type, and a 7-speed unit with deep crawler and overdrive ratios. A separate lever engaged the crawler gear and with practise a skilled driver could use that ratio to split the remaining six gears.

Aware that both owners and drivers of lorries were becoming more discerning, Leyland provided hydraulic power assistance to the Marles cam and double roller steering gear used on new Octopuses.

Octopus braking systems were up-graded from those of '24' series lorries. Air pressure actuation was retained, of course, as by 1960 it had become the industry's standard for most top quality heavy lorries. Cam operation was used incorporating Bendix-Westinghouse slack adjusters. Wider brakes were fitted, with 4.5 inches wide shoes on the first axle, and 7 inches wide components on the third and fourth axles. They acted against reduced diameter brake drums of 15.5 inches. Such drums were better for withstanding braking pressure and they were also ribbed for additional strength and improved cooling. Total footbrake area was 1,002 square inches, with 758 square inches of parking brake on the back wheels activated by an air-assisted, mechanical pull-on handbrake.

A pressed steel drivers' structure fabricated by Motor Panels of Coventry completed the distinctive appearance of a Power-Plus Octopus. Leyland dubbed it their Vista Vue cab, and it was a long door development (for retracted front axle) of the famous L.A.D. cab. A lightweight version with glass fibre outer panels was also made available for Leyland Beavers and Octopuses as an option and it saved about 2 cwts. It was not a popular choice with customers due to concerns about strength and durability, and not many were sold. Rather surprisingly a heater was considered a luxury item once again; heating and demisting could be provided at extra cost during manufacture, or the customer could choose to provide this essential facility later.

With lightness in mind Leyland's engineers used a slightly thinner and fractionally less deep chassis frame for both haulage models assembled with non-reactive suspensions. Other Octopus variants retained earlier chassis dimensions. All rigid suspension lorry chassis were flitched in the rear bogie section to reduce stresses. A 36 gallons fuel tank was hung on the chassis, and this could be increased to 48 gallons capacity on haulage lorries. Tyres were still 9.00 x 20 size, 12 ply rating for home market eight-wheelers and 11.00 x 20, 12 ply covers for export models.

Many pre-1960 Octopus lorries were destined to remain in service for several years to come, especially the hundreds in service as tankers with oil companies and bulk liquids hauliers. Nevertheless, Leyland now had a completely new range of eight-wheelers available with more specification options than ever before for both existing and potential customers.

Power-Plus Octopus models with Vista Vue cabs were only in production for a relatively short period of just under five years. During that time some important specification changes were implemented, mainly concerned with weight saving measures that resulted in additional models.

In the year 1962 a lightweight Leyland Octopus model was announced, which was separate to the existing line-up and was a standardised lorry for the home market. Designated chassis type 24O.14R it had a wheelbase of 16 feet 6 inches and as a flat platform vehicle it was very light at approximately 7.25 tons unladen. This allowed a hefty 16.75 tons payload.

Only the O.600 Power-Plus engine was available for this Octopus, with either a 5 or 6-speed gearbox. Similarly, only the non-reactive bell crank rear bogie could be specified, but different double drive, hub reduction axles were fitted. These were comparatively lightweight units made by Albion Motors, which of course was a wholly owned subsidiary company of Leyland Motors. The standard overall axle ratio was 6.25:1, with either an alternative lower gearing of 7.712:1, or higher one of 5.555:1.

Burman re-circulating ball type steering gear was used on the lightweight Octopus. It had a variable ratio that reduced the effort needed by the driver to turn the steering wheel when manoeuvring his heavily loaded lorry. There was no hydraulic power assistance provided.

As well as using the lightweight Albion axles, more weight saving was achieved by designing a lighter chassis frame. Also, the glass fibre panelled Vista Vue cab was fitted, but the steel panel option was available if desired. If the latter was chosen an additional 2 cwts was added to the tare weight.

The following year, 1963, saw a lightweight Octopus tipper added to the range. It had a wheelbase of 14 feet 9 inches with an identical specification to its longer wheelbase stable mate. Typically, with an aluminium alloy body the tipper tared off at 7.75 tons for a legal payload of 16.25 tons. The glass fibre cab was discontinued because of customer opposition to the concept.

To accommodate this new Octopus tipper, the 24O.14R model became 24LWO.1R, with identical wheelbase and specification as before, and the tipper was designated type 24LWO. 2R.

Power-Plus Octopus lorries provided higher engine outputs, but some of Leyland's legendary reputation for reliability was lost in the quest for extra power. Some O.680 engines were prone to cylinder head gasket failures until modifications were introduced. The Vista Vue L.A.D. cab was not universally popular and attracted criticism because it was a noisy and cramped working environment for a long distance lorry driver.

With the introduction of Annual Testing and Plating in 1969, many users of '24' series and Power-Plus Octopuses investigated means of uprating braking systems to meet new legislation. Leyland Motors provided technical information and conversion kits for all its air-braked lorries. Providing brakes were well maintained Octopuses from both model ranges could usually meet interim braking standards applicable between 1969 and 1972 without too much difficulty. To comply with final standards after 1972 service brakes on the second steering axle were necessary. An independent secondary air system controlled with a hand valve, separate air reservoir, and multi-diaphragm brake chambers was also essential. The vast majority of '24' series Octopuses were withdrawn from service after final braking standards became compulsory because the newest were some 12 years old by then. However, some operators of them such as Hipwood & Grundy decided to carry out these braking system modifications.

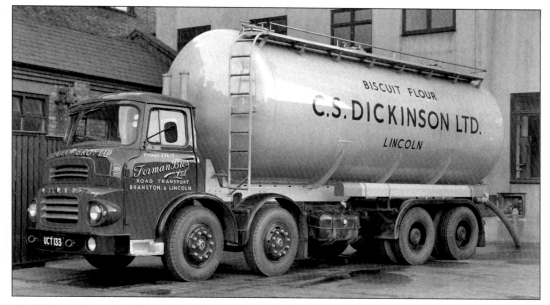

By 1962 L.A.D. cabbed Power-Plus Octopus eight-wheelers were entering service. Forman Bros. Ltd had this flour tanker on contract to miller C.S. Dickinson Ltd. of Lincoln. The tank had a capacity of 16 tons of biscuit flour and was a twin-ram tipper with pneumatic fluidising discharge. Note the new hub reduction rear axles.

Also in service with a flour miller was this short wheelbase Octopus grain carrier, operated by King Bros, a wholly owned subsidiary of Wm. Nelstop Ltd., long established Stockport miller. It had Pilot Works twin-ram tipping gear with stabilisers, and it was photographed in Smith's Road, Darcy Lever, quite close to Pilot's factory at Bolton.

A high capacity van and trailer capable of carrying over 3,000 tins of biscuits. In 1962 most biscuits were still sold loose in grocer's shops by the pound weight. The Octopus ran regularly between Reading and Liverpool and it was operated by the Associated Delivery Co. who also built the bodywork.

Specialist fish haulier Donnan placed this Octopus into service in 1963 for the express transport of fresh fish from English and Scottish ports to the main wholesale markets. It had a demountable refrigerated container. An additional large capacity fuel tank was also fitted on the offside to permit long distances to be covered from Scotland to Billingsgate, London, without re-fuelling en route.

This was an innovative dual-purpose body on Charrington's Octopus. It could be used as both a tipper and tanker. In tipper mode it hauled coal to London, and by using a Portolite synthetic rubber tank, (made by Marston Excelsior of Wolverhampton), inside its body, it could return to Coventry with 3,600 gallons of oil, which it was loading in this picture taken in 1962.

Almost 30 years had passed since the first Octopus TEW (see Section 1) bought by Ingham & Tipping entered service, and in 1963 the Bamber Bridge company was still loyal to Leyland Motors. Its specialist bulk grain carrier could legally carry 15 tons payloads with the single compartment body built locally by Fowler of Leyland.

L.A.D. Octopuses were very popular tankers and Chesterfield based Kennings Ltd. covered south Yorkshire and the East Midlands distributing petroleum products on behalf of Shell-Mex and B.P. Ltd. A couple of 4,000 gallons capacity spirit tankers were loading product at a fuel terminal.

Orbit Petroleum Ltd. was one of the smaller regional fuel suppliers and distributors, sourcing its supplies from one of the major oil companies. It ran on 'C' Licence. The driver was "doing the dips", to prove to the purchaser that the compartment had been emptied. This practice is now outlawed for health and safety reasons. Note there were no safety guards on the catwalk of the tank. Nowadays such tankers are bottom loaders, with no necessity to climb on top at any time.

In 1963 there were four Octopuses in service with Preston Borough Council, all with high capacity domestic refuse bodies that were either compactors, or were equipped with walking floors for discharging purposes. They conveyed refuse from the town to the banks of the River Ribble, near Freckleton. Being a tidal estuary, nature disposed of the rubbish into the Irish Sea.

A lightweight L.A.D. Octopus (note the smaller rear axle hubs) that was one of several in service with Richard Biffa on waste haulage. Again it had a capacious body and the driver was somewhat precariously removing the retaining net from the load before tipping. Such front ledges were potentially very dangerous in wet weather.

In its heyday Leyland Motors was a large exporter of vehicles in CKD format along with vast quantities of components and spare parts. Fleet number 51 with the Works Transport department was an L.A.D. Octopus photographed in King Street, Leyland, with a very high load of crated components for export.

Leylands were very popular with both own account fleets and haulage contractors in and around Sheffield, where virtually every load was a maximum weight one of steel. Brightside Foundry had this early L.A.D. Octopus that entered service in 1962 seen here with a load of castings.

A fine shot of an Octopus making a turn, leaving Western Dock at Dover. Andrews of Bristol made its 3,300 gallons tank for Pfizer.

Operated by W.B. Russell on contract to the Clyde Portland Cement Co. of Glasgow, this short wheelbase Octopus was photographed in 1963 delivering to a large construction site. Its dual containers were made by Portasilo Cement Tanks and each could hold 239 cubic feet of cement.

J.H. Whitehead & Co. Ltd. of Turton, near Bolton, and the local body builder, Pilot Works, thought up an innovative method of carrying furnace coke. The Octopus was equipped with three aluminium alloy demountable skips, each with a capacity of 945 cubic feet of coke. The lorry collected coke from County Durham and delivered it to Leyland Motors foundry at Farrington.

Hall & Co. had a large fleet of tippers engaged on sand and gravel haulage in the Home Counties and London. This aggregate bodied Octopus was seen on a building site in 1964, where excellent traction provided by Leyland's double drive rear bogie was a massive advantage in difficult conditions frequently encountered with such deliveries.

Southport Sand Co. was part of W. Rainford (Liverpool) and their Octopus was being loaded in the sand dunes at Southport. Most of this sand was destined for foundries in Lancashire, the Black Country, and West Midlands. An older '24' series Octopus was waiting to load when this picture was taken in 1964.

There was a maximum weight load of hardcore on this Octopus of Lowland Sand & Gravel Company, photographed on a dry and dusty day in 1966. Note the prominent strengthening cross-members on its aluminium alloy body. Twin-ram tipping gear was specified.

Before the advent of global brewing groups Guinness had the world's largest brewery at Dublin, from where its production was exported worldwide. To keep the brewery supplied with malt and hops required a huge fleet of lorries, and Leylands were prominent for many years. This Octopus was carrying a demountable bulk malt body made by Craven Homalloy, and this usually remained in place for 9 months of the year. For the rest of the time the eight-wheeler carried casks of the famous stout.

Albion Fuel Oil was based off Gallowgate in Glasgow, and its new unregistered Octopus was about to enter service in 1964. Unusually for a tanker of this type the lorry's own diesel tank was still on the nearside chassis rail. Photographed at the Regent fuel terminal, this became Texaco in 1967.

SECTION 4

Freightline And Other Ergomatic Cabbed Types

By 1964 the British road transport industry was still regulated by legislation enacted over thirty years before, with relatively minor amendments in the meantime. Just as the 1933 Road and Rail Traffic Act had transformed matters, then new statutes laid down in 1964 (and later in 1968) were equally far-reaching and revolutionary. Ironically, it had been the 1933 act that had brought the rigid eight-wheeler into being, but the 1964 Construction and Use Regulations hastened its demise as a frontline general haulage lorry. Great Britain was now becoming pro-articulated lorry for maximum gross weight duties, as artics could legally run at 30, and even 32, tons from 1965. Eight wheelers gained a marginal increase of 2 tons to 26 tons gross weight, but for reasons explained shortly most new rigid eights remained at 24 tons. The logic for encouraging articulated lorries to proliferate was hard to fathom.

Traditionally, British commercial vehicles had been exported in quantity to countries that were part of the old Empire, and remained constituents of the Commonwealth. There were anomalies of course; several South American and Middle Eastern states also bought British vehicles. Reasonable sales levels were also being won in some European countries, and politicians at home were advocating closer trading ties with Europe for the future prosperity of the nation. Eventually the pro-European lobby won the day with Great Britain joining the Common Market in the early 1970s. However, in much of Europe in 1964, heavyweight artics were seen less frequently than they were here, because rigid four-wheelers pulling drawbar trailers ruled the roost on long distance runs.

Whilst an increase in gross vehicle weights, coupled with new axle spacings and overall vehicle lengths had been anticipated, and indeed lobbied for, by lorry builders, many aspects of the 1964 Construction and Use Regulations were unexpected and took the industry by surprise. From about 1963 new vehicles had been made with future weight increases in mind and some types could comply with the new legislation, others were unable to do so.

Eight-wheelers were in the latter category and this was because a totally different, longer, wheelbase was required to meet axle spacing and overall length limits for 26 tons gross weight operations. Rigid eights assembled from 1965 able to operate at the higher weight were long, unwieldy, and awkward to manoeuvre. Consequently most new eight-wheelers remained at 24 tons, being easier lorries to drive. The days of eight-wheelers as mainstays of general haulage fleets were over as they were replaced by new articulated vehicles capable of carrying 20 to 22 tons loads, up to 4.5 tons more than even a 26 tonner rigid eight. It was not the complete end of the type, of course, because eight-wheeler tippers and tankers remained popular with specialised hauliers.

Leyland Motors announced and displayed its new heavy goods vehicle range for complying with amended Construction and Use Regulations at the 1964 Commercial Vehicles Show. They were marketed under the Freightline banner and the most obvious change was a striking new cab, which had been designed by the studios of Michelotti. This was the Ergomatic cab and it also tilted to allow access to the lorry's engine. This trend setting cab has been described in *The Leyland Beaver* and other titles within "The Commercial Vehicles Archive Series".

At that time manufacturers used the Commercial Vehicle Show for announcing models that were still several months away from production, so Freightline Leyland Octopuses did not appear on the roads until late 1965. Right or left hand control lorries were available. The modern Power-Plus Octopus driveline and specification was retained, except for lightweight versions which were deleted for the time being. One important new feature was fitting brakes to the second steering axle. Revised chassis designations were introduced as recorded in Appendix A.

Both 24 and 26 tons Octopuses could still pull drawbar trailers at 32 tons gross train weight, but that emotionally stirring sight virtually disappeared from roads overnight as the articulated lorry revolution gained ground.

The Leyland Octopus model designed for 26 tons operations had a 20 feet 9 inches wheelbase and was shod on 10.00 x 20 tyres. This chassis permitted almost 30 feet of flat platform body space. With lightweight non-reactive bell crank bogie suspension its tare weight was approximately 8.5 tons, depending on the body materials. This gave a possible legal payload of 17.5 tons, but it was reduced by 0.5 tons if rigid rear suspension was specified. There was no trailing fourth axle option listed.

An Octopus for 24 tons also had a new wheelbase dimension of 15 feet 9 inches, which could be for a haulage, tipper, or tanker body. Again, the operator could order either lightweight 4-spring or rigid 2-

spring bogie suspension. With the former and flat platform body an unladen weight of about 8.25 tons allowed a payload of 15.75 tons. The tipper version permitted a load of some 15.25 tons, depending on the body's construction. If the heavier rear suspension was chosen payloads were reduced by 0.5 tons and only double drive axles were available.

With brakes now being provided as standard on the second axle the total braking area increased to 1,246 square inches. The parking brake area and hand braking actuation remained the same as before.

There were no changes to the basic air braking system and power assisted Marles cam and double roller steering was retained. Chassis frame depth, width, and thickness measurements were as for Power-Plus models, but of course there was a much longer frame for the 26 tonner Octopus.

By 1968 operators and lorry builders had gained experience of running heavier lorries at higher speeds. New sections of Motorways were opening every few months and the majority of hauliers decided that more powerful engines were preferable for sustained fast running. Fears had been raised that higher horsepower would equate to poor fuel consumption figures, but in the hands of a good driver the converse was often true. Consequently, the O.680 unit became the standard fitment in Freightline Octopuses. At about this time the "O" engine prefix was discontinued from most data lists and the engine types became either 600 or 680.

Also in the year 1968 lightweight versions of Leyland Octopuses re-appeared. (26LOT and 24LOT etc.) Once again they were standard specifications and all concurrent Octopus wheelbases and variants could be ordered in lightweight format. They were much the same in concept as Vista Vue cabbed models, with Albion double drive, hub reduction axles and non-reactive bell crank 4-spring suspension.

Weight savings were impressive with 10 cwts being saved on the long wheelbase 26 tons gross weight chassis, making 18 tons payloads possible. Even greater weight reductions were made to shorter wheelbase lorries, which had 0.75 inch shaved off their chassis frame depth. In total 12 cwts was saved and payloads were correspondingly increased by this amount.

Only the 200 bhp 680 engine was fitted, mated to either a 5-speed direct top, or 6-speed overdrive gearbox. Standard rear axles ratio was 6.25:1, with optional lower and higher gearing available.

The following year, 1969, saw the lightweight 26 tonner Octopus model being discontinued. Very, very few of these machines were sold. For less cost than a chassis-cab Octopus a customer could buy a top weight Leyland Beaver tractive unit and semi-trailer. Furthermore the artic was more flexible in operations and could carry heavier loads.

In this same year the remaining lightweight 24 tons Octopus models were granted a few more options. The 5 or 6-speed gearboxes could be either wide or close ratio versions. An exhaust brake could be specified, and 10.00 x 20 14 ply tyres were available if desired. The haulage variant also received a slightly deeper chassis frame.

Adwest power assisted steering gear became standard and Butec electrical components replaced CAV alternators, starter motors, and regulators.

Leyland took a decision that was surprising to Octopus operators in 1970. It discontinued production of these acclaimed eight-wheelers. Such had been the move to articulation by lorry operators that the eight-wheeler market was small in comparison. For the next five years Leyland had no eight-wheeler of its own in its catalogue, an unthinkable situation at one time. However, it is believed that some Octopus chassis were occasionally completed on the insistence of long-standing customers. The British Leyland Group, as the parent company was by then, was well served by other marques in any case. AEC was still building heavyweight Mammoth Major Eights, and also lightweight Marshal 8s, (see *The AEC Mustang & Marshal)*; Scammell was assembling it popular and relatively light Routeman models, which also used Leyland 680 engines; and Guy Big J8 rigid eights were still available. Both Scammell and Guy offered proprietary engine options including Rolls Royce, Gardner, and Cummins.

Towards the end of 1975 Leyland was keen to promote a new Octopus range once more. There were several reasons why their earlier decision had been reversed. The eight-wheeler market had latterly experienced something of a revival with an increase in gross weight to 30 tons in 1972. Whilst such lorries would never again feature as mainstream general haulage vehicles, they were still popular as tippers and tankers. Another niche use for them, and a relatively new one, was as brick and building block carriers with lorry mounted cranes. Another era, that of hand loading 6 - 7,000 bricks onto a lorry was ending, as quicker, easier, and safer methods were explored. A 30 tonner eight-wheeler with its own crane was perfect for the job. A good 20 tons payload could be carried and a rigid eight performed better on building and construction sites than an articulated lorry.

British Leyland was also gradually phasing out production of AEC and Guy lorries, so two competing marques would eventually be no more. Finally, Leyland itself had been developing its new 500 Series lorries, and after a lengthy, difficult gestation period its innovative fixed cylinder head engines were thought to be achieving acceptable reliability.

However, what proved to be the remaining five years of Octopus production saw various engines being used. But in 1975 a virtually new model was specified, with very little carried over from Freightline versions and far more proprietary components than ever before used in their construction. This was partly a consequence of the massive financial problems the parent group was then experiencing.

One major item obviously retained from 1970 was the Ergomatic cab, although it was face lifted externally and re-trimmed internally. It was also raised by 5 inches to be known as the high-datum version. This was done to enable larger radiators to be fitted and to improve airflow around engines, again for better cooling. One drawback with these cabs as originally mounted was inadequate engine cooling in certain circumstances with bigger engined, more powerful models.

These 500 Series Octopuses were for 30 tons gross weight and two wheelbases were available. A 21 feet 0 inches version for haulage duties permitted 26 feet 6 inches of body space and was an incredibly light machine, weighing approximately 8.25 tons with aluminium alloy flat platform body. A profitable 21.75 tons payload was feasible. Even the 19 feet 0 inches wheelbase tipper model offered about 21.25 tons loads with a typical body.

Power came from a Leyland fixed head 502 six-cylinder turbocharged engine of 500 cubic inches capacity, or 8.2 litres. With a bore of 118 mm and stroke of 125 mm it produced 205 bhp at 2,400 rpm and torque of 542 lbs. ft. at 1,400 rpm. The development of this interesting engine series will be studied in a subsequent volume in "The Commercial Vehicles Archive Series", along with the lorries they were used for.

The clutch was a bought-in component from Lipe-Rollway. It was a twin dry plate design with clutch brake and 14 inches diameter plates operated hydraulically. Similarly, the gearbox was from another manufacturer, namely Fuller and its RTO 609 unit was used. It was a 9-speed constant mesh, range-change type with overdrive top gear. There was provision for either high or low torque power takeoffs.

A double drive rear bogie, assembled around Albion double drive, hub reduction axles with a lockable third differential, completed the driveline. It was given a 19 tons load rating. Various final drive ratios were available depending upon application. Standard gearing for the haulage chassis was 6.933:1 for a governed top speed of 56 mph, and the tipper model was lower geared at 7.712:1 for 50 mph top speed. Higher and lower ratios could be specified for each model.

It is worth noting that references are made to a 500 Series Octopus model with 8 x 2, trailing fourth axle specification in 'World Trucks No. 14, Leyland' by the late, highly respected Pat Kennett. It is doubtful if many, if indeed any, were built to this configuration, and all specification data sheets found by Neil Mitchell for the author are for 8 x 4 lorries.

Leyland reverted to 2-spring suspension for its new Octopuses, but it was a much lighter version than that of earlier models. It was a fully articulated design with inverted taper leaf springs pivoting on rubber-bushed trunnions. Four rubber-bushed radius arms located the axles. Anti-slew brackets with renewable wear plates completed the arrangement.

Each front axle was rated for 6.5 tons, but only plated for 6.0 tons. Long, semi-elliptic springs were assisted by shock absorbers. The four front wheels had recirculating ball type steering with integral power assistance, plus an auxiliary power ram on the steering relay lever.

Bigger brakes than before were necessary for heavier loads, so these lorries used 6 inches wide shoes on every wheel. Drum diameter was 15.5 inches to give a total braking area of 1,360 square inches.

Activation methods differed, with front axles utilising fixed cam, sliding shoes. Rear brakes also had a fixed cam arrangement, but with one leading and one trailing shoe. The air pressure circuit was divided for safety reasons; axles one and three were braked together, as were axles two and four. This enabled the mandatory secondary braking system to be either half of the main footbrakes circuit. Spring brakes on every axle except the first comprised the parking brakes. A graduated hand control valve was the means of actuation.

A strong chassis frame 12 inches deep and 3 inches wide made from steel almost one third of an inch thick was the basis of a 500 Series Octopus. Tipper chassis were strengthened with two external flitches per side member, whereas haulage models had an inverted 'L' flitch plate on each side. All versions had additional flitching in their rear bogie bays. Tippers had 50 gallons fuel tanks hung on chassis, and haulage models received 75 gallons capacity tanks.

Tubeless tyre sizes were D22.5 (11 x 22.5) on every wheel, with optional E22.5 (12 x 22.5) covers available if required. This choice allowed an operator to plate the Octopus front axles at their design weights of 6.5 tons. Finally, Butec electrical components were used.

A more powerful engine option was offered in 1976. It was the same basic fixed head 500 unit but now tuned to develop 230 bhp at 2,400 rpm with 612 lbs. ft. of torque. This was known as a Leyland 511 engine. The clutch, and transmission, remained unchanged but top speeds were increased by making a 6.25:1 rear axles ratio standard for the haulage model, and 6.933:1 gearing was applied to the tipper. Either model could have these alternative ratios fitted and a third, lower option of 7.428:1 was also available.

Minor improvements to the cab interior and trim were carried out and these applied to Leyland 502 powered Octopuses.

In spite of continuing development work on Leyland fixed head 500 engines poor reliability remained a constant feature and the company was forced to abandon what proved to be a very costly engine design. Leyland had to revert to modernised versions of older, tried and tested engines that were up-dated in remarkably short development programmes with strictly limited financial budgets. Given these circumstances they served the company well.

The first of these modernised engines to be used in Octopus chassis was the normally aspirated Leyland L12 in 1977. This was a development of AEC's proven AV760 unit of 12.4 litres, or 761 cubic inches. It retained the former engine's bore and stroke dimensions of 136 mm x 142 mm. A Bosch 'P' type in-line injection pump was used to produce 203 bhp at 2,200 rpm with 570 lbs. ft. of torque at 1,400 rpm. Turbo-charged versions of this unit were used in contemporary Leyland Marathon models, and later Leyland T45 Roadtrains.

Irrespective of the poor reputation suffered by Leyland 500 engines, there was another motive for using what to all intents and purposes was still an AEC engine in an Octopus. Competing AEC Mammoth Majors, which had been around slightly longer than Octopuses, ceased production at Southall in August 1977. In an attempt to persuade loyal Mammoth Major customers to purchase Octopuses it obviously made sense to use some AEC designed components.

Nor was it just the engine that was AEC based in L12 Octopuses. The 17 inches diameter single plate clutch, with air assisted hydraulic actuation, and gearbox were traditional AEC designs. This latter unit was a version of those D203 6-speed constant mesh overdrive gearboxes that had originally been made by Thornycroft at Basingstoke. By the time they were fitted into Octopus chassis the Leyland Group had disposed of its Basingstoke plant to Eaton who continued to make gearboxes for Leyland and sister companies.

Apart from engines and gearboxes L12 Octopuses retained all other features of 500 Series eight-wheelers. Because an L12 engine was 5 cwts heavier than a Leyland fixed head 500 unit there was a corresponding loss of payload. Adjustments were made to rear axles ratios to compensate for slightly less torque and lower revs with L12 engines. The standard gearing for the haulage model was still 6.25:1 for 56 mph top speed, but the tipper was lower geared at 7.428:1 for 47 mph governed top speed. Alternative gearing, ranging from 5.555:1 highest ratio to 7.712:1 lowest, could be specified for both versions.

By the late 1970s Leyland was pinning its future hopes for recovery on a totally new range of goods vehicles which were under development with code T45. Volume production was planned for 1981. In the meantime some revamping of existing models was carried out leading to an Octopus 2 description being applied to eight-wheelers announced in late 1978. By then the Ergomatic cab, which had been a trendsetter in 1965, was outdated and looking its age. But it still had to serve for another couple of years.

There was not a lot of difference between Octopus 2 models and their immediate predecessors, except another engine option was offered. The L12 variant remained much the same apart from some standardisation of rear axles ratios to 6.25:1 for both tipper and haulage chassis. Lower geared alternatives could be chosen if preferred.

Customers now had a choice of a Leyland TL11A power unit in place of a L12 engine. This TL11A unit was a lightly turbo-charged modernisation of Leyland's long-serving O.680, which it will be recalled had its origins in the wartime period of the early 1940s. In its latest incarnation it was tweaked to produce 209 bhp at 2,200 rpm and 605 lbs. ft. of torque at 1,300 rpm. A Sigma in-line fuel injection pump was fitted.

Completing the driveline of a TL11A powered Octopus 2 was a Lipe-Rollway LP twin dry plate hydraulic clutch and Fuller RTO 609 9-speed constant mesh overdrive range-change gearbox. The clutch had a brake to facilitate rapid gear changes. Rear axles ratios were identical to those of L12 chassis.

And so, towards the end of the year 1980 the final orders for Octopus 2 chassis were completed at Leyland. Except for a few years in the Second World War, and again during the early 1970s, these distinguished eight-wheelers had been in production for nearly 46 years. If those made in that final period lacked the charisma of earlier models they nevertheless maintained Leyland's tradition of building these imperious lorries and being a leading exponent of the type.

With the availability of new Leyland T45 models in 1981 the Octopus name was discontinued. In its place came the Constructor, developed and assembled by Scammell at Watford. For a few years to come there would be Leyland input into Constructors as TL11 engines continued to be fitted.

It was late 1965 before the first Ergomatic cabbed Freightline Octopuses entered service. C. Clutton & Sons owned abattoirs at Wrexham and Liverpool and this tilt-cabbed Octopus had a refrigerated van body for distributing hanging meat to wholesale markets and butchers. The eight-wheeler was a 24 tonner and the refrigeration unit was a Thermo-King.

This photograph illustrates perfectly the long wheelbase necessary to comply with 26 tons gross vehicle weight legislation under the latest Construction and Use Regulations applicable in 1966. The aluminium alloy dropside body was 30 feet long. The Octopus was registered in Dorset.

A couple of 24 tons gvw Octopuses newly into service with Stirling County Council in 1967. They were equipped with Edbro twin-ram tipping gear and insulated double skin bodies, capable of carrying hot tarmac, built locally by Munro of Chapelhall. They were the first lorries in this fleet painted in a new bright yellow livery with black stripes on the tailgates for safety reasons at roadworks.

Steetley Minerals operate quarries in south Yorkshire, Derbyshire, and Nottinghamshire and a short wheelbase Freightline Octopus was new in 1967. The company ran a large fleet of Leylands for many years. With a well-sheeted load this would have been high quality foundry sand.

Here was another method of carrying and delivering special types of sand for foundries and chemical plants processing sand for its silica content. British Industrial Sand Ltd. favoured powder tankers with pneumatic discharge by 1966, as many of its large customers had installed storage silos. Because sand is heavy a short wheelbase Octopus and relatively small tank was sufficient for a 15 tons payload.

A classic example of legal regulations not being entirely appropriate for some uses. Concentrated Sulphuric Acid is a dense, heavy liquid and to get maximum load onto an eight-wheeler a 2,000 gallons capacity tank was large enough. Consequently Imperial Smelting, a subsidiary of Rio Tinto Zinc, had to order a long wheelbase 26 tonner Octopus and fit it with a narrow tank to be legally compliant.

Scottish Agricultural Industries was another committed Leyland user. Its long wheelbase Octopus was photographed unloading at Heathhall Store, Dumfries, where feed and fertilizer was stored after being trunked from its mills and plants at Glasgow, Leith, or Ayr. Leyland and Albion four-wheelers usually carried out deliveries to farms in Dumfriesshire and neighbouring counties.

Liverpool tipper operator, L.F. Briggs (1932) Ltd. had an unusual job with its 1968 Octopus. The load was imported round timber destined for Bryant & May Ltd., match manufacturers. Once processed, there would have been countless thousands of matchsticks in this load.

Roughdales Brickworks of St. Helens was at the forefront of modernising brick deliveries in 1967, by equipping its 26 tonner Octopus with a crane. Both loading and unloading was much quicker and safer with mechanical methods as opposed to traditional manual handling. The driver controlled the crane with a wander lead. The cradle for supporting the jib when the crane was not in use was clearly visible behind the cab.

Carrying a 'Super Octopus' badge, this was a fixed head 511-engined Octopus, with 'Super' being used for a short time to denote the most powerful, turbo-charged version. By 1977 brick and block carrying lorries were invariably equipped with cranes, in this instance an Atlas type, made at Blackwood, Lanarkshire. Brickhaul's Octopus was for 30 tons gvw and its wheelbase was very similar to Roughdales' 26 tonner, a further C. & U. Regulations revision having taken place in 1972.

With competing eight-wheelers from within the Leyland group having been axed by late 1977, the Octopus range enjoyed healthy sales figures for some time. They were light and competitive although certain engine options were unreliable. Animal foods producer Nitrovit Limited had a large fleet of Octopuses and Bison six-wheelers, and this single ram tipper was typical of its operations.

An Octopus on contract to Tinto Sand & Gravel Co. in 1978. Tinto excavated deposits in south Lanarkshire and it was a main supplier of aggregates to Motorways construction companies in Central Scotland.

Amoco had a substantial presence in the British oil and petroleum market from the early 1970s until the 1980s, when it sold its interests here to BP. It mainly operated AEC lorries, but after the demise of that marque in 1977 it purchased equivalent Leyland models. This 1978 Octopus spirit tanker was powered by an AEC derived Leyland L12 engine.

Compacting refuse bodies employ complex hydraulics, as shown in this photograph, and they are also expensive. Allen Morgan Plant (Ilkley) Ltd. placed this Octopus 2 into service in 1979, towards the end of production of a world famous eight-wheeler range. Its exhaust stack was mounted upright to keep it out of harm's way on rough tips and landfill sites.

SECTION 5

Leyland Octopus In Retrospect

Analyse the heyday of eight-wheelers on British roads and it was roughly no more than twenty years in the mid-twentieth century. This might surprise most lorry connoisseurs because these imposing vehicles are rightly regarded as indicative of road transport in Great Britain at its most romantic. By the time first generation rigid eights were becoming established World War Two curtailed production. But from the mid-1940s for the next twenty years the eight-wheeler was king of the road, and Leyland Octopuses were most numerous. This chassis and axles configuration was a British eccentricity and whilst some were exported to Australia, New Zealand, South Africa and a few other countries, numbers were smaller than other types of lorries.

The 1950s was the period when eight-wheelers were in the ascendancy. If they were Leylands and AECs they often pulled drawbar trailers. Other rugged eight-wheelers made by Foden, Atkinson, and ERF lacked sufficient power from Gardner engines for long distance trailer work. Miserly bosses did frequently saddle frugal Gardner 6LWs (with only 112 bhp) with trailers, but they were hard work and how those drivers yearned for a Leyland Octopus with 150 bhp from its O.680 engine. Ask any eight-wheeler driver from that era what his preference was and he will usually reply "Leyland Octopus or AEC Mammoth Major".

Those of us who were young enthusiasts in those days recall scenes indelibly printed in our mind's eye. Let me share one with you. The local Radcliffe Paper Mill had a 22.O/1 Octopus and trailer. What a sight it made loaded with large reels of brown paper two high, expertly sheeted and roped. I was only eight years old or so when I first saw it northbound on the A1 near Catterick, when Fred Holden, with whom I was riding in a Bedford S-type, overtook it. I later discovered it was heading for Hugh Stephenson's packaging factory at Darlington. Driver and mate were two elderly, tiny men to my eyes, yet there they were with this huge lorry and trailer. They could have been brothers, even twins, but they and that Octopus were inseparable for years. As far as I know no photograph of that lorry exists, yet its image is as clear to me today as it was nearly fifty years ago. A definitive road haulage scene of those years.

Consider next the blue chip transport fleets that purchased Leyland Octopuses when they were archetypal market leaders. Regular, repeat orders were received from such as British Road Services, Esso Petroleum, Shell-Mex and B.P., Spillers Milling, London Carriers, John Summers, and J. & A. Smith to name only a few. Prestigious customers that knew what they wanted. Such was the reliability, ruggedness, and longevity of '22' and '24' series Leylands they had no need to seek alternatives. These lorries might have been basic and slow, but my goodness they were dependable and durable, but remember, they were designed and well engineered for the work they had to do in the conditions and roads appertaining at the time. And how well they did it lasting up to 15 years in service in many instances. Even then they weren't finished, many of them were snapped up by travelling showmen for fairground service. A sure attestation to quality, reliability, and longevity.

Leyland engines and drivelines were in the main ultra reliable until the advent of fixed head 500 series engines, but these hardly impacted upon Octopus sales as by then eight-wheeler demand had dwindled. Some problems were experienced with early O.680 Power-Plus engines as the demands for additional power created unexpected weaknesses. Modifications eventually eradicated failures. The Leyland O.600 unit and its O.680 derivative rightly rank amongst great British diesel engines of last century. Testament to the soundness of their fundamental design was the turbo-charged TL11, a development that lasted into the 1980s and over 40 years since inception. These renowned Leyland engines were also used in contemporary Scammell, Albion, Bristol, and Foden lorries. A couple of noted continental commercial vehicle manufacturers, namely Scania-Vabis and DAF used basic O.600 and O.680 engine designs, along with Leyland engineering expertise, for developing into their own turbo-charged derivatives. Hotchkiss in France also had association with Leyland Motors.

Vista Vue, L.A.D. cabbed Octopuses also have their aficionados. Who can ever forget seeing one of those operated by H. B. & H. of Newton-le-Willows in action with a twin-wheeled drawbar trailer on a dolly behind it? The legality of such an outfit was challenged for a time, but was found to be valid. In truth the L.A.D. cab was not very popular with drivers and operators and its rapid replacement by Ergomatic cabbed models was welcomed. Main complaints about the Vista Vue were high noise levels, lack of space, and the undeniable fact that it was used on a premium quality (and priced) lorry, but it was similar to those fitted to Dodge lorries, a cheaper make.

Freightline Octopuses only reigned for a short period at a time when eight-wheelers were endangered by legislation that favoured articulated lorries. Usually they were reliable in service and any problems were mainly caused by engines overheating. A fault dictated by smallish radiators and poor airflow as a consequence of the cab being universally designed for numerous Leyland Group models of varying carrying capacities and engine sizes. From a driver's perspective the Ergomatic cab was superior to anything that had been used previously. By providing different driveline and rear bogie options, coupled with lightweight chassis versions, Leyland ensured that with Vista Vue and Freightline models any customer should have been able to satisfy his operational needs, no matter how demanding.

By the time Leyland re-entered the eight-wheeler market under its own name, the company was starting a long battle for survival. It was a desperate period and warranty claims for fixed head 500 series engine failures cost it dear. In the end the engine was discontinued and there are those who would say it was the engine that bankrupted Leyland. It was certainly one of several contributory factors. Those 500 Series, L12, and TL11A Octopuses were stopgaps until new Scammell Constructor models appeared. L12 and TL11A models were good lorries and were amongst the lightest eight-wheelers on the market. A commendable trait of Leyland rigid eights that dated back to the very first TEW8 model in 1934/5.

It is difficult to convey just what a great and successful company Leyland Motors was before the early 1970s to those who only knew it after that date. It produced world-class commercial vehicles renowned for top quality, reliability, and value for money. Octopus eight-wheelers in this country's nostalgic, "golden age", of road transport were more than worthy of that accolade.

The Leyland Octopus for most of its lengthy production life was a definitive British eight-wheeler lorry.

Little is known about this photograph, except the location was Leyland Motors South Works, probably in the 1950s judging by the already ancient cement mixer. The Octopus was a short wheelbase '24' series twin-ram tipper, of unknown ownership, but it could have been a company demonstrator on account of its pristine body interior. Note the position of the spare wheel behind the cab.

Based at Farnworth, Lancashire, Hipwood & Grundy operated a sizeable fleet of Octopus tankers on black oil and bitumen haulage. These Leylands gained almost cult status because of their longevity, with the last 24.O/4 tankers not being withdrawn until 1981 when they were well over 20 years old. They were virtually anonymous with little or none sign writing. This one was photographed discharging bitumen at Asphaltic's roofing felt factory in Wigan. (Photo: Author's collection from Neville Brydon)

A. Naylor Ltd. of Tipton bought a new L.A.D. Octopus with dropside body in 1962. Even at that date mirrors were quite small, providing very limited rearward vision for a driver

It was April 1971 when these two Octopuses were photographed waiting to discharge Ilmenite, which is beach mined mineral sand. The location was probably a railhead or wharf at Fremantle, Western Australia. (Photo: Ron Knight from Tony Petch)

This L.A.D. Octopus of Waikato Bitumen was hauling that liquid when photographed at Bombay, near Auckland N.Z. in 1977. Note the length of the trailer drawbar, the positioning of the vertical exhaust stack to keep exhaust fumes away from road surfacing gangs, and the super single tyres on the rear axles. It had an O.680 engine with 6-speed gearbox plus crawler. Resting on the fuel tank was a bag of potatoes, bought by the driver at a market garden just over the crest of the hill! (Photo: Rufus Carr)

Zarb Transport serves the Australian sugar industry and their L.A.D. Octopus and trailer was carrying molasses. It had an O.600 engine with a 6-speed gearbox and ran as an 8 x 2 lorry with the fourth axle diff blanked off. The location was Mackay, Queensland in 1979 when the Leyland was 16 years old and still a frontline lorry. (Photo: Rufus Carr)

Octopuses in Australia and New Zealand had to work hard for their keep, as shown by Ward's of Gisbourne L.A.D. Octopus and trailer. It had an O.680 engine and 10-speed gearbox, and was equipped with Domett livestock decks and Jensen crates. Laden with sheep it was resting at Waiocka Gorge, N.Z. in 1973. (Photo: Rufus Carr)

This L.A.D. Octopus was one of a large fleet of British lorries operated by mining company D.F.D. Rhodes Pty. Ltd. in Western Australia. It was hauling manganese ore from Woodie Woodie mine to Port Headland in December 1964. The roads were so poor and rough that hydraulic tipping gear was not fitted because the equipment would have disintegrated before journey's end. Instead, the side boards were lowered and the ore was pushed off with a front end-loading shovel.   (Photo: Joe & Laura Harrison from Tony Petch)

Any mention of famous Scottish Leyland operators must include Charles Alexander & Partners (Transport) Ltd. of Aberdeen. They were engaged on several road haulage disciplines over the years, but were famed for high-speed fresh fish transport in days before refrigeration was widely used. In 1966 their new Freightline Octopus was loading fish on a Lancashire Flat demountable body, and the lorry was painted in a recently introduced metallic blue livery.

This 26 tonner Freightline Octopus entered service with Allied Feeds in Australia in 1969. With its long wheelbase it was an ideal chassis for mounting three bulk bins. They had bottom discharge equipment and were similar to British Tollemache designs. Even so, maximum payload was achieved with a short drawbar trailer. (Photo: Young & Richardson from Tony Petch)

Although unlettered, this 24 tonner Freightline Octopus tipper was operated by a firm called Glendinning. It had a marine ply wooden body, built in house, using metal frames. It generally ran out of Linhay Quarry, Ashburton, Devon, hauling limestone for road making and agricultural purposes.

A purposeful looking Freightline Octopus and trailer for hauling aggregates and gravel that was based at Tauranga depot in North Island N.Z. in 1974. It had a fairly standard specification of O.680 engine with 6-speed plus crawler gearbox. (Photo: Rufus Carr)

Zarb Transport once again and one of their Freightline Octopus and trailer outfits for hauling raw sugar in Mackay, Queensland. This company remained faithful to British lorries for many years, but favoured cheaper, basic specifications and low horsepower for work on relatively flat terrain. This Leyland had an O.600 engine with 6-speed gearbox and it was built with a trailing axle rear bogie courtesy of a BPW fourth axle. Zarb Transport had heavily modified lorries to reduce weight and only operated during the sugar harvest between June and November each year. When not in use their fleet was parked under cover in huge sheds. ((Photo: Rufus Carr)

A fine Freightline Octopus and trailer taking a load of sheep on their final journey to Southdown Meat Works, Auckland N.Z. in 1971. It had O.680 engine with 6-speed plus crawler gearbox. (Photo: Rufus Carr)

An even longer than standard wheelbase 26 tonner Octopus converted for airport refuelling duties in 1968. The chassis was stretched by a further 3 feet and the tank was 31 feet long by 10 feet at its widest, and it was 11 feet high. Known as a 'London' tanker it was built by Shell and Thompson of Bilston. The lorry's tank could hold 9,000 gallons of jet fuel and it also pulled a 7,000 gallons capacity trailer for a gross train weight of 80 tons. A Pneumo-Cyclic semi-automatic 10-speed gearbox was fitted and the tanker's purpose was refuelling newly introduced Boeing 747 Jumbo jets.

Wimpey operated one of the larger Octopus 500 series and Octopus 2 fleets in the late 1970s and early 1980s. This company had been a huge AEC and Leyland operator for decades. Here an Octopus L12 was reversing under a hopper at a tarmac plant in 1978.

APPENDIX A
Leyland Octopus Chassis Details

DESIGNATION	WHEELBASE Ft. Ins.	GROSS WEIGHT	ENGINE	YEAR	NOTES
TEW8D	16' 10"	22 Tons	8.84L petrol / 8.6L C.I. (oil)	1935	Double Drive (Worm) Bogie
TEW8T	16' 10"	22 Tons	8.84L petrol / 8.6L C.I. (oil)	1935	Trailing Axle (Bevel) Bogie
TEW9D	18' 10"	22 Tons	8.84L petrol / 8.6L C.I. (oil)	1935	Double Drive (Worm) Bogie
TEW9T	18' 10"	22 Tons	8.84L petrol / 8.6L C.I. (oil)	1935	Trailing Axle (Bevel) Bogie
TEW11	15' 10"	22 Tons	8.84L petrol / 8.6L C.I. (oil)	1937	Double Drive (Worm) Bogie
TEW12	17' 10"	22 Tons	8.84L petrol / 8.6L C.I. (oil)	1937	Double Drive (Worm) Bogie
TEW14T	15' 11"	22 Tons	8.84L petrol / 8.6L C.I. (oil)	1937	Trailing Axle Bogie Std. Gearbox 1938
TEW15T	17' 11"	22 Tons	8.84L petrol / 8.6L C.I. (oil)	1937	Trailing Axle Bogie Std. Gearbox 1938
TEW14D	15' 11"	22 Tons	8.84L petrol / 8.6L C.I. (oil)	1938	Double Drive, (Worm) 4-spring Bogie
TEW15D	17' 11"	22 Tons	8.84L petrol / 8.6L C.I. (oil)	1938	Double drive, (Worm) 4-spring Bogie
22.O/1	17' 9" Haulage	22 Tons	O.600	1946	Optional O.680 engine from 1951
22.O/3	15' 6" Tipper, Tanker	22 Tons	O.600	1946	Optional O.680 engine from 1951
24.O/4	17' 9" Haulage	24 Tons	O.600 / O.680	1955	Air Brakes
24.O/5	15' 6" Tipper, Tanker	24 Tons	O.600 / O.680	1955	Air Brakes
24O.9R	17' 0" Haulage	24 Tons	O.600 / O.680 Power-Plus	1961	Vista Vue 4-spring Bogie
24O.10R	14' 9" Haulage, Tanker	24 Tons	O.600 / O.680 Power-Plus	1961	Vista Vue 4-spring Bogie
24O.11R & L	17' 0" Haulage	24 Tons	O.600 / O.680 Power-Plus	1961	Vista Vue 2-spring Bogie
24O.12R & L	14' 9" Haulage, Tanker	24 Tons	O.600 / O.680 Power-Plus	1961	Vista Vue 2-spring Bogie
24O.13R & L	14' 9" Tipper	24 Tons	O.600 / O.680 Power-Plus	1961	Vista Vue 2-spring Bogie
24O.14R	16' 6" Haulage, Tanker	24 Tons	O.600 Power-Plus	1962	Vista Vue Lightweight
24LWO.1R	16' 6" Haulage, Tanker	24 Tons	O.600 Power-Plus	1963	Vista Vue Lightweight
24LWO.2R	14' 9" Tipper	24 Tons	O.600 Power-Plus	1963	Vista Vue Lightweight
26OT.1R & L	20' 9" Haulage	26 Tons	O.600 / O.680 Power-Plus	1965	Freightline 4-spring Bogie

DESIGNATION	WHEELBASE Ft. Ins.	GROSS WEIGHT	ENGINE	YEAR	NOTES
24OT.15R & L	15' 9" Haulage, Tanker	24 Tons	O.600 / O.680 Power-Plus	1965	Freightline 4-spring Bogie
24OT.16R & L	15' 9" Tipper	24 Tons	O.600 / O.680 Power-Plus	1965	Freightline 4-spring Bogie
26OT.2R & L	20' 9" Haulage	26 Tons	O.600 / O.680 Power-Plus	1965	Freightline 2-spring Bogie
24OT.17R & L	15' 9" Haulage, Tanker	24 Tons	O.600 / O.680 Power-Plus	1965	Freightline 2-spring Bogie
24OT.18R & L	15' 9" Tipper	24 Tons	O.600 / O.680 Power-Plus	1965	Freightline 2-spring Bogie
26LOT 1CR	20' 9" Haulage	26 Tons	680 (Power-Plus)	1968	Freightline Lightweight
24LOT 2CR	15' 9" Haulage, Tanker	24 Tons	680 (Power-Plus)	1968	Freightline Lightweight
24LOT 3CR	15' 9" Tipper	24 Tons	680 (Power-Plus)	1968	Freightline Lightweight
24LOT.2DR	15' 9" Haulage, Tanker	24 Tons	680 (Power-Plus)	1969	Freightline Lightweight
24LOT.3DR	15' 9" Tipper	24 Tons	680 (Power-Plus)	1969	Freightline Lightweight
30T502/30TF2	19' 0" Tipper, Tanker	30 Tons	502	1975	500 Series Octopus
30T502/30LF2	21' 0" Haulage	30 Tons	502	1975	500 Series Octopus
30T511.30TF2	19' 0" Tipper, Tanker	30 Tons	511	1976	500 Series Octopus
30T511.30LF2	21' 0" Haulage	30 Tons	511	1976	500 Series Octopus
30TL12.30T2	19' 0" Tipper, Tanker	30 Tons	L12	1977	L12 Octopus
30TL12.30L2	21' 0" Haulage	30 Tons	L12	1977	L12 Octopus
30TL12.30T2	19' 0" Tipper, Tanker	30 Tons	L12	1979	L12 Octopus 2
30TL12.30L2	21' 0" Haulage	30 Tons	L12	1979	L12 Octopus 2
40T11A 30TF2	19' 0" Tipper, Tanker	30 Tons	TL11A	1979	TL11 Octopus 2
40T11A 30LF2	21' 0" Haulage	30 Tons	TL11A	1979	TL11 Octopus 2

Notes.

1. "L" suffix applied to chassis designations for Power-Plus and Freightline Octopuses indicates that left hand control versions were available for export markets. Vista Vue L.A.D. and Ergomatic cabs were hardly suitable for adaptation to left hand control, so export figures for these models were low.

2. The year given in the above data signifies when new, or re-specified models were generally available for customers. New models in particular were announced in the autumn of the preceding year.

APPENDIX B

Octopus Engine Details

Pre-1939 engine power outputs have been corrected to a common database, which is British Standards AU:141 1967 rating. This is to provide meaningful comparisons with later engines. BS testing results were standardised at 60 degrees Fahrenheit temperature and 29.92 inches of mercury atmospheric pressure. Brake horsepower quoted is nett power transmitted by the flywheel after deducting that absorbed by engine auxiliaries. For further comparison with modern metric bhp values increase quoted figures by 9%.

ENGINE	CYLS.	BORE x STROKE INCHES	CAP. Cu. Ins.	RAC H.P.	BORE x STROKE MILLIMETRES	CAP. cc	BHP	@ RPM	TORQUE Lbs. Ft.	@ RPM	YEAR	NOTES
8.84L Petrol	6	4.56 x 5.5	540	50.0	115.9 x 139.7	8,840	115	2,200	360	1,000	1934	OHC layout
8.6L C.I. (oil)	6	4.5 x 5.5	525	48.6	114.3 x 139.7	8,595	93	1,900	305	1,300	1934	OHC layout
8.6L C.I. (oil)	6	4.5 x 5.5	525	48.6	114.3 x 139.7	8,595	106	1,900	330	1,200	1938	Re-tuned OHC
O.600	6	4.8 x 5.5	597	N/A	122.0 x 139.7	9,800	125	1,800	410	900	1945	WW2 design
O.680	6	5.0 x 5.75	677	N/A	127.0 x 146.0	11,100	150	2,000	450	1,100	1951	Developed O.600
O.600 Power-Plus	6	4.8 x 5.5	597	N/A	122.0 x 139.7	9,800	140	1,700	438	1,200	1961	Power-Plus
O.680 Power-Plus	6	5.0 x 5.75	677	N/A	127.0 x 146.0	11,100	200	2,200	548	1,200	1961	Power-Plus
502	6	4.65 x 4.92	500	N/A	118.0 x 125.0	8,200	205	2,400	542	1,400	1975	500 Series
511	6	4.65 x 4.92	500	N/A	118.0 x 125.0	8,200	230	2,400	612	1,400	1976	500 Series
L12	6	5.37 x 5.59	761	N/A	136.0 x 142.0	12,473	203	2,200	570	1,400	1977	Developed AV760
TL11A	6	5.0 x 5.75	677	N/A	127.0 x 146.0	11,100	209	2,200	605	1,300	1979	Developed O.680

NOTE: Leyland 600 and 680 engines as listed from about 1968 were identical to O.600 and O.680 Power-Plus units respectively.